THUS SPOKE LAOZI

THUS SPOKE LAOZI

A New Translation with Commentaries of

— DAODEJING —

Charles Q. Wu

University of Hawai'i Press
Honolulu

Foreign Language Teaching and Research Press
Beijing

21 20 19 18 17 16   6 5 4 3 2 1

Library of Congress Cataloging-in-Publication Data
Laozi, author.
  Thus spoke Laozi : a new translation with commentaries of Daodejing / Charles
Q. Wu.
    pages   cm
  In English and Chinese.
  "Original edition published by Foreign Language Teaching and Research Press"—
Title page verso.
  Includes bibliographical references and index.
  ISBN 978-0-8248-5640-3 (hardcover : alk. paper)
  ISBN 978-0-8248-5641-0 (paperback : alk. paper)
  1. Taoism.   2. Taoist philosophy—Early works to 1800.   I. Wu, Charles,
translator, writer of added commentary.   II. Laozi. Dao de jing.   III. Laozi. Dao de
jing. English.   IV. Title.
  BL1900.L26E5 2016
  299.5'1482—dc23
             2015031939

To my wife, Diane D. Ma

Contents

Acknowledgments

I would like to take this opportunity to honor the memory of Professors Shui Tiantong, Xu Guozhang, and Wang Zuoliang, who gave me the keys to the beautiful garden of English language and literature. I would also like to honor the memory of my Columbia mentor, the late Professor Karl Kroeber, who taught me "not what to think but how to think" and let me explore the possibility of a Daoist reading of the Wordsworthian imagination. After I finished my PhD, Professor Kroeber continued to encourage me to delve deeper into the subject, but I changed my field from English to Chinese studies.

It was at this juncture that my old friend Chen Huixian emerged to show me the wonders of *qigong*, a newly revived legacy of the Daoist tradition. She introduced me to many of her students and invited me to teach the philosophical underpinnings of *qigong* at her workshops. Like the "best student" that Laozi mentions in chapter 41 of *Daodejing*, Ms. Chen's students not only diligently studied the principles of *Dao* but put them into practice in their quest for a better life for others as well as for themselves. These and others who have heard my lectures are all my teachers, to whom I owe a great deal.

On my journey to share my understanding of *Dao*, I was fortunate to get to know Professor Zhan Shichuang of Sichuan University, the most prolific scholar on Daoism in China. He and I collaborated in leading a study tour to Daoist mountains and temples in China. His presentations were both insightful and inspiring, as his academic works are richly informative and creatively conceived.

Among the friends who joined this tour was Brenda Nielson, a lady who has done in-depth study of Daoism and written screenplays and novels on cross-cultural experiences. Brenda proved to be most helpful as a consultant as well as a cheerleader for this project of mine.

Another adviser I feel deeply indebted to is the Chinese historian Lynn Connor. She and I share a common interest in the Daoist symbolism of classical Chinese gardens. Lynn has a schoolteacher's meticulousness in reading my drafts and giving me timely feedback.

A heartfelt thank-you goes to the leaders and staff of the Foreign Language Teaching and Research Press, who generously accepted my manuscripts and brought the book to its present finesse. I especially appreciate the high-quality professionalism and friendly cooperation of my copy editor, Ms. Meng Jiawen.

Thanks are also due to renowned calligrapher Mr. Ma Yizhao, who made available details from his ancestors' artworks for us to use as illustrations for this book.

Of course I would not have been able to deliver this long drawn-out project without the loving patience and care of my wife, Diane D. Ma, to whom I dedicate this book.

Introduction

With so many English versions of the *Dao De Jing*, why another?

— Moss Roberts (2001), *Laozi: Dao De Jing: The Book of the Way*, p. 2

The *Daodejing* has probably been translated into the English language more often than any other piece of world literature. Why translate it again?

— Roger Ames (2003), *Dao De Jing: "Making This Life Significant":
A Philosophical Translation*, p. ix

If eminent sinologists like Professors Ames and Roberts have to provide a "reasonable answer" to the same "reasonable question" for their translations, there is no excuse for this much belated attempt to be exempted from the same password test. I don't have a newly discovered manuscript to justify my new translation. Nor do I claim a fresh angle from a specific discipline. But the infinite profundity and consequently the infinite translatability of Laozi's immortal work always make it possible to bring the readers yet another step closer to what Laozi actually says and how he says it through still another translation aided by commentaries. Arguably what Laozi actually says is very much a matter of interpretation, but equipped with my line-by-line bilingual text and commentaries, readers will be able to have the aha moment to say, "Now

I know what Laozi is saying." In this introduction I would like to lay out my approach to some of the perennial issues that all translators have to face.

Authorship

To understand Laozi and the book he is believed to have authored in historical context, the biggest challenge lies in the scantiness of verifiable information about the dates and life of the author. Without getting into the ramifications of the subject, I rely, as many scholars do, mainly on the biographical account in the monumental *Records of the Historian* by Sima Qian (c. 145–90? BCE), the Han dynasty historian. According to this account, Laozi's name was Li Er or 李耳, styled Dan or 聃. He was a native of Quren Village, Lai Township, Ku County of the Kingdom of Chu, and a keeper of the royal archives of the Zhou dynasty. Laozi was around twenty years older than Confucius (551–479 BCE), and the two met when Confucius was about thirty years old. So Laozi must have lived, like Confucius, at the junction of two historical periods in Chinese history known as the Spring and Autumn Period (770–476 BCE) and the Warring States period (475–221 BCE). Those were the turbulent times when feudal states were at war with one another and the Zhou dynasty was in decline. Diverse concerned thinkers came forth with remedies of all stripes for the troubles of the time, thus creating the golden age of "polemics among a hundred schools of thought" in the intellectual history of China. Among these different schools of thought, two stood out to be the most influential: the one led by Confucius and the other by Laozi. As Sima Qian puts it at the end of his biographical notes on Laozi, "Those who learn from Laozi put down the teachings of Confucius, and those who follow Confucius also put down Laozi."

As a serious historian, Sima Qian does not exclude the possibility of other candidates for the mysterious Laozi. But he makes it clear that these versions are mere hearsay by inserting the phrase 或曰 (*huò yuē*) meaning "some say" or "it is said" in his narrative. For instance, he says, "It is said that Laozi lived over a hundred and sixty years. Some say he lived over two hundred." "Some say Dan or 儋 was Laozi; some say not." By contrast, Sima has no such reservations when telling the story of Li Er. He even lists the names of the descendants in Laozi's lineage all the way down to his own time. He concludes his biography of

Laozi by reaffirming that "Li Er practiced Non-doing and let people transform themselves. He remained tranquil and let people find the right course."

As for Laozi's authorship of the book by his name, Sima Qian seems to have no qualms including in his official biography the legend that when Laozi was on his way to seclusion through the Hangu Pass, the pass keeper Yin Xi persuaded him to leave behind his teachings in writing, which came to be the immortal five-thousand-character classic known first as *Laozi* and later as *Dao De Jing* (henceforward *Daodejing*).

In insisting on the historicity of Laozi, I try my best to resist the temptation of using mythical material that had been grafted onto his little-known life after he had attained the posthumous status of deity. At the same time I try to develop through my translation and commentaries a persona that voices all the beliefs and concerns in the five-thousand-word text. There is no denying the universal value of Laozi's teachings that transcend space and time. I especially value their applicability to our own life experience in the twentieth and twenty-first centuries. However, I try my best not to use anachronistic examples to illustrate Laozi's teachings or use his teachings to analyze modern-day events. While acknowledging the inevitable subjectivity of interpretation or translation, I believe it is only appropriate to leave it to the readers to relate the ancient teachings to their own experience.

Editions

The version of *Daodejing* in wide currency to this day consists of eighty-one chapters divided into two parts, with the first thirty-seven chapters as part 1, *Dao*, and the rest as part 2, *De*. This basic structure, with all its slight variations, may be traced back to two major compilers-commentators, one under the pseudonym He Shang Gong (Lord of the River), dated around 200 CE, and the other, the infant prodigy Wang Bi (226–249). While the Lord of the River's line-by-line commentaries place equal importance on governance of the state and cultivation of the individual, Wang Bi's metaphysical interpretation helped establish his edition as the master text as well as the **received version** of *Daodejing*, from which numerous variations and commentaries have stemmed down the centuries.

However, no manuscripts of this classic were known to be extant until 1973, when a much earlier pair of transcripts of *Daodejing* on silk was unearthed in an ancient tomb at Mawangdui near Changsha, the capital of Hunan Province. The silk script had two slightly different versions: Text A may have been copied anywhere between c. 206 and 195 BCE, and Text B copied c. 194–180 BCE. Despite many errors of the copyists and the corruptions of the material, these are the earliest complete manuscripts seen by modern readers. They not only confirmed the existence of the Daoist classic but solved some of the textual issues in Daoist studies. One striking difference between the Mawangdui version and the received version is the reverse order of the two parts, with the *De* part placed before the *Dao* part in both versions of the Mawangdui text. This discovery led to the publication of a new translation titled *Lao-tzu: Te-Tao Ching—A New Translation Based on the Recently Discovered Ma-wang-tui Texts*, by Robert Henricks (1989). Nonetheless, the received version continues to prevail as the source of new translations, while the Mawangdui manuscripts are often referenced as a significant place to go for textual and interpretative verification.

Twenty years after the Mawangdui trove was excavated, an even earlier, though excerpted, version of *Daodejing* inscribed on bamboo strips was found in 1993 in the ancient tomb at Guodian near the city of Jingmen, Hubei Province. This discovery placed the date of the earliest script around 300 BCE. What especially intrigued scholars in the field was a new text, beginning with the sentence "太一生水 (Tài Yī Shēng Shuǐ)," or "The Great One Gives Birth to Water," included in the last of the three bundles of strips that recorded excerpts from *Daodejing*. However, while this new document deserves renewed attention and may indeed throw new light on the classic itself, the value of the Guodian *Daodejing* is limited by its fragmentary nature. Nonetheless, it is an eloquent validation of the proximity of the classic to the supposed date of creation by its supposed author. It has also served as another good source of reference when an ambiguity or debate occurs.

Without claiming originality, I use the Wang Bi edition of eighty-one chapters with its numerous commentaries as the basis of my translation and interpretation. For textual verification I also consulted the Mawangdui and Guodian scripts and other variations. For interpretation I checked He Shang Gong's line-by-line commentaries, among others. But my main source of information is Professor Chen Guying's revised edition of *Laozi* with notes and commentaries (Beijing, 2009). In fact I followed his redaction quite closely and benefited immensely from the many historical commentaries he cites. The choice of any specific interpretation or editorial decision is mine. I cite other reliable sources selectively, but since my target audience is non-academic and non-Chinese readers, I would rather not bother them with all the ramifications of textual preferences.

Getting It

Throughout its history *Daodejing* has been read variously as a book on philosophy and metaphysics, a religious scripture, a classic on self-cultivation, an advisory on governance, a foundational text on military strategy, an encyclopedia of practical wisdom, a pre-Christian prophecy, and so forth. While all these readings are possible, their validity depends on the basic understanding of three key concepts: *Dao* or 道, *De* or 德, and *wuwei* or 無爲.

If the whole text of *Daodejing* may be divided into two parts, as has been verified by the Mawangdui silk scripts, albeit in reverse order of the received version, it is amazing that the *Dao* part and the *De* part both begin with a negative definition, namely, what is **not** (the eternal) *Dao* and what is **not** (the superior) *De*. This fact suggests that the terms *Dao* and *De* were already in currency in Laozi's time and that he wanted to make sure from the outset that the way he used these terms would not be confused with the common usage. But nowhere in the text does Laozi attempt to give a comprehensive, abstract definition of either concept. His is the strategy of a fiction writer giving an incremental description of the different aspects of the protagonist's character as the story unfolds. This is especially true of his characterization of *Dao*.

The word *Dao* appears in at least thirty-six chapters of *Daodejing*, often more than once in one chapter. Among these, chapters 1, 21, 25, and 42 are perhaps the most crucial in that they directly address the large issues of *Dao* as the ultimate source and motive force of the universe, of its infinity and mobility, its intangibility and ineffability, and above all its relevance to us, the "ten thousand things." If you have a good grasp of the essence of these chapters, the rest of the book will make good sense.

Sinologists and translators have to this day tried hard to find an equivalent in English for *Dao*. The first success they had, or came close to, was the biblical "Way." It is true that the literal meaning of *Dao* is "way," or "road." But when Jesus says in John 14:6, "I am the way, and the truth, and the life," he proclaims, "No one comes to the Father except through me." On the other hand, *Dao*, according to Laozi, **is** the ultimate Almighty, the Mother of all things and not just the "way" **to** something else. The solution of this discrepancy has led to one of the greatest contributions to the English language, that is, the addition of the word "Tao," now spelled "Dao," from which are derived "Taoism" and "Taoist," to the English vocabulary. I readily accept this "translation" as many of my predecessors have done, reserving, however, the leverage of the literal alternative, "way."

The next key word in *Daodejing* is of course *De*. Although there are sixteen chapters in which the word appears, its configuration is much less clear than that of *Dao*. This vagueness is not without good reason because *De* is simply the emanation or realization of *Dao*. As Laozi puts it at the beginning of chapter 21, "The behavior of the Great *De* follows that of *Dao* and *Dao* alone." All that one has to do is follow the ways of *Dao*, and there is *De*. In that sense, the word should not be interpreted, or limited in its interpretation, only as "moral integrity" or "virtue," a usage that was already prevalent in Laozi's time. However, many translators still use the word "virtue." Arthur Waley calls it "Power," perhaps in the etymological sense of "virtue" as "virility." *De* was also a eulogistic term to refer to the meritorious governance of a feudal ruler. To avoid such conceptual ambiguities, I decided to use the transliteration *De* the way we have accepted *Dao*. But I keep the word "virtue" where Laozi critiques the popular use of the word. In grappling with the meaning of *De*, one needs to be aware that the character *De* or 德 is homonymous and, indeed, interchangeable with the character *de* or 得, meaning "get," "receive," "obtain," or "attain." Laozi must have this other *de* in mind when he talks about *De* in reference to attaining the *Dao*, or simply "getting it." For evidence of the interconnectedness between the two *des*, one may take a close look at chapter 38, where the character 德 appears in nine lines, and then at chapter 39, where 得 is the key word in seven lines.

When Laozi was exploring the different dimensions of *Dao* and ways to attain it, he was not merely engaging in some idle metaphysical discourse. The times he lived in did not allow such luxury. What he was looking for was an infallible model by which all human troubles, be they social, political, or personal, could be resolved. He found this model in *Dao* itself or, if you like, in Nature, or the Universe, which *Dao* mothers. The benchmark of this model is not proactive, not aggressive, not the silver bullet but, on the contrary, non-active and non-contentious. In the words of the English romantic poet William Wordsworth, it is "wise passivity." In Laozi's vocabulary it is *wuwei* or 無爲 or "not doing" or "Non-doing." The term was not Laozi's invention but had been around in his time like *Dao* and *De,* though not as widespread. The expression appears only once in the Confucian *Analects* but in at least ten chapters of *Daodejing.* Pay special attention to chapters 48 and 63. The idea of *wuwei* is central to Laozi's philosophy because it embodies his practical wisdom based on his vision of the workings of *Dao* as the source of all power and wisdom.

"Not doing" is a state of "being" as well as a way of getting things done. Put briefly, it means freeing oneself from one's self-will and following the natural ways of *Dao*; it means getting everything done with the best effect and least effort and cost. Translators have tried to incorporate the rich meaning of *wuwei* in their quest for equivalents, resulting in such renditions as "do nothing coercively," "no conscious action," "non-action," "inactivity," "(act) without effort," and so on. I have tried to find a one-size-fits-all solution, but like attempts by other translators, the "one size" is too limiting and does not always fit well. I also want to avoid using modifiers that are not in the original phrasing. After much experimentation, I came to the conclusion that the best way is, in Daoist fashion, to go back to the crude, unmodified, paradoxical "not-doing" and, with a little tweak, "Non-doing," as a parallel to "Nonbeing." Sometimes I switch to the verb phrase "do nothing" where the context permits.

Style

One of the hallmarks of Laozi's rhetoric is the frequent use of paradoxes. It is a feature that is deeply embedded in Laozi's incisive discernment of the ironies of the world. He describes this feature as "a truthful statement that sounds like its opposite." It reveals a universal phenomenon that what seems absurd may very well be true. Examples are plenty, such as "Great music has little sound," "Great image has no form," "The sage puts himself in the rear and finds himself in front."

Just as frequently as he uses paradoxes, Laozi often resorts to common-sensical analogies drawn from his thoughtful observations of natural phenomena. For instance he compares the "highest Good" to water "because water brings good to all things and does not contend." He likens the art of governing a large state to "cooking a small fish" because the fish, being small and delicate, has to be treated tenderly and not stirred too much. These analogies are very convincing and serve as important supplements to the intellectually more challenging paradoxes.

Another manifestation of Laozi's literary genius is his poetry. By poetry I do not just mean verse, but also his succinct prose style. In fact it is not always easy to tell apart his prose from his verse. Many of his prose statements, such as "The journey of a thousand *li* begins under your feet," have become immortal mottoes for posterity. But the verse makes his teachings especially memorable, and the rhymes help readers determine where a sentence ends and where a line belongs. This is particularly important because in classical Chinese there is usually no punctuation to facilitate the reading process. Part of Laozi's poetics is parallelism or repetition whereby either a syntactical pattern or a word is repeated throughout a stanza. Such repetitions accentuate the poet's emphasis and make indelible impressions on the reader's memory.

Translation and Commentaries

All translators struggle for a balance between fidelity to the spirit and letter of the original text on the one hand and readability of the translation to native speakers of the target language on the other. This balance is especially challenging when it comes to translating a classic like Laozi's *Daodejing*, for what we see here is not only a book of ideas but a book of poetry, a work of literary art. My strategy is to retain as much as possible the original literariness so that the readers can hear, as it were, through my translation, what Laozi sounds like as if they were reading him in Chinese. The beauty of Laozi's language, defining as well as reflecting the beauty of his thinking, would be lost if what English readers have access to is merely a prosaic paraphrase. Of course, much of the original beauty is doomed to be lost in translation, particularly the rhymes. I don't even attempt to mimic any of those because, as I have seen in some of the translations of

Chinese poetry, such attempts can only result in a bunch of clever jingles. The one thing I do not want to do and, fortunately, am not in a position to do is to produce a translation that sounds more like Elizabethan poetry than an authentic translation. I urge my readers to step a little bit out of their comfort zone to appreciate the unfamiliar cadence of a different literature, albeit still through a readable translation. The good news is that there is such a thing as poetic license, even in one's native literature.

As a supplement to the translation, I have attached a commentary to each chapter whereby I explain textual and interpretive issues, especially those that involve some key Chinese characters that have multiple meanings or are homonymous with other characters. The task I set myself is to provide the historical and linguistic contexts for a proper understanding of some of the knotty points. In doing so I may serve as a tour guide but claim no finality. Instead of presenting my readers with a ready-made, well-packaged product and claiming that is what Laozi says and that is all you need to know, I invite my readers to participate in the translation and interpretation as an open-door, open-ended process. At the same time I try my best to avoid letting my words overshadow those of Laozi. Listen to what Laozi has to say first, mull over it, and then read the commentary in case you need some aid or clue, with which you may or may not agree. Hopefully this process will also yield the by-product of providing the readers with some exposure to the Chinese written language both through the bilingual text proper and the presence of Chinese characters in the commentaries.

Simplified versus Traditional Characters

Chinese characters have gone through millennia of evolution. The form known as the simplified characters was adopted by the People's Republic of China in 1956 and has become the standard in the mainland of China and Singapore. The form that was the norm prior to that has been dubbed the complex or traditional characters. This form is still the standard in Taiwan, Hong Kong, and Macao and is widely used in the Chinese diaspora. Chinese classics are still printed in traditional characters in mainland China, but there is a growing trend to use simplified characters. The *Daodejing* text in this book is printed in both forms.

Pinyin

All the characters that appear in the commentaries as well as in this introduction are accompanied with their phonetic spelling known as Pinyin. A Romanization system for Chinese characters known as the Wade-Giles system has been in service for more than a century. It is a phonetically based system with its own rationale and has served the English publishing world well. It was under this system that the word "Tao" came into the English language, following the rule that the letter *t* before a vowel letter stands for the unaspirated *t* as the *t* in "style," as opposed to the *t* followed by an apostrophe (t'ao), which should be pronounced like the English consonant *t* as in "tower." Likewise, the apostrophe is used to distinguish aspirants like *p'* and *k'* from their unaspirated counterparts as in "spell" and "skill." By this rule, the character 德 should be spelled as *te* in Wade-Giles because the *t* is unaspirated. In 1958, the People's Republic of China published a new Romanization system known as Pinyin, literally "phonetic spelling." Actually the new system is structured quite closely according to the old Wade-Giles, but with at least two major differences.

One is the sweeping elimination of the apostrophe to let *p*, *t*, and *k* instead of *p'*, *t'*, and *k'* be pronounced as aspirants while the Roman letters *b*, *d*, and *g* are admitted into the system for the unaspirated *p*, *t*, and *k* in the old system. Thus *Tao* became *Dao* and *Te* became *De*. The pronunciation has not changed. It's the spelling.

The second major change is the use of *c*, *ch*, *q*, *x*, *z*, and *zh* to represent Chinese phonemes unfamiliar to English speakers. The letter *c* is pronounced like the sound "ts"; *ch* is pronounced like a thick "ch" sound with the tongue curled up; *q* like a thin "ch" sound as in "cheek"; *x* like a thin "sh" sound as in "sheep"; *z* like the sound "ds" or "dz"; and *zh* like a thick "dr" sound with the tongue curled up. Related is the letter *i* after *c*, *ch*, *q*, *x*, *z*, and *zh*, representing the prolongation of the consonant that precedes it. Thus the sound *zi* in the name "Laozi" is pronounced like "dzzzz."

A lesser but important change is the replacement of the Wade-Giles *j* with the letter *r*. Thus the Confucian value 仁 (humaneness, or benevolence) should be spelled as *ren* instead of *jen*. At the same time, the letter *j* is restored to its regular role of phonetic representation in English such that people now know

"Beijing" should sound like "beidging" and not "beizhing." That also explains the spelling of "Jing" in *Daodejing*.

Despite some early resistance due to force of habit and political divisiveness, after the PRC resumed its seat in the United Nations in the 1970s as a permanent member of the Security Council, the adoption of Pinyin became inevitable. Today the Pinyin system is internationally in use to the extent that the Library of Congress and well-established sinologists have switched to it, although a reluctant few, along with the older publications, still stay with the old Wade-Giles. Hopefully this dual existence will phase out.

Part One:
Dao

1

道可道，非常道；名可名，非常名。无名，天地之始；有名，万物之母。

故，常无，欲以观其妙；常有，欲以观其徼。

此两者，同出而异名，同谓之玄。玄之又玄，众妙之门。

道可道非常道	Ways may be spoken of as *dao*, but they are not the eternal *Dao*;
名可名非常名	Names may be cited as names, but they are not the eternal name.
無名天地之始	Nameless is the beginning of Heaven and Earth;
有名萬物之母	Named is the Mother of all things.
故	Thus,
常無欲以觀其妙	Through eternal Nonbeing, one observes its mystery;
常有欲以觀其徼	Through eternal Being, one observes its manifestations.
此兩者同出而異名	The two have the same origin but differ in names;
同謂之玄	Both may be called profound.
玄之又玄	Profound and still more profound
众妙之門	Is the gateway to all mysteries.

COMMENTARY

You don't have to know Chinese to see the character 道 (pronounced *dào*) occurring three times in the very first line of the chapter. The etymology of the word, as many scholars have pointed out, suggests a "path," "road," "pathway," or simply "way" leading to a place. But by the time the book known as *Laozi* was written, the word had already been used by thinkers of different stripes to refer to an ill-defined but all-encompassing higher order. Apparently Laozi was reacting to both meanings of the character in contemporary use. At the same time he must also be aware of a derivative usage of 道 as a verb meaning "to speak of." English translators have adopted two different strategies to convey the metaphysical sense of the word 道: one by borrowing the biblical use of "the Way" as in "I am the way, and the truth, and the life" (John 14:6) and the other by borrowing the Chinese word, originally spelt as *Tao* according to the Wade-Giles system of Romanization (hence Taoism and Taoist) and now as *Dao* (hence Daoism and Daoist) in the Pinyin system. The present translation tries to honor the long-since naturalized word *Tao* or *Dao* in the English language while acknowledging the more physical sense of "way" or "ways" as well as the verbal derivative "to speak of." Thus, the first of the three 道 refers to the various "ways" proposed by Laozi's contemporary thinkers to fix the social malaise of the time; the second 道 takes on the verbal meaning of "to speak of" or, more specifically, "to speak of something as *dao*"; and the third 道 refers to the eternal *Dao*.

In terms of syntax, most English translators tend to treat the first line as one sentence: "The way that can be spoken of is not the eternal Way." The Mawangdui version breaks the line into two parallel sentences, each ending with a sentence-ending particle 也 (*yě*). The present translation follows this syntax but stays with the received version that does not have the particle 也. This reading makes it easier to spell out the different meanings of the character 道 in translation.

In the next line, Laozi stands from the height of the eternal and debunks the mundane emphasis on "names." Confucius for one urges the "rectification of names" as a prerequisite for all moral and political discourse, but Laozi thinks naming names belongs to the business of the mundane world. What interests him is the nameless world of the "eternal," which is the basic meaning of the character 常 (*cháng*) in the received version. The Mawangdui version uses the synonym 恒 (*héng*) meaning "constant," "invariable," or "eternal." This substitute precludes from the present context other meanings of 常 such as "often," "frequent," or "ordinary."

The negative 無 (*wú*) meaning "to not have" or "to not exist/be" and the affirmative 有 (*yǒu*) meaning "to have" or "to exist/be" form an antithetical pair. Thus, 無名 (*wú míng*) means "have no name" whereas 有名 (*yǒu míng*) means "have a name"; 無欲 (*wú yù*) means "have no desire," and 有欲 (*yǒu yù*) means "have desires." But both 無 (*wú*) and 有 (*yǒu*) gain ontological status when they refer respectively to the states of "Nonbeing" and "Being." You have to be aware that classical Chinese has no punctuation and its meanings may vary depending on how you punctuate or where you pause as you read. Thus, you can punctuate lines 3 and 4 of the first stanza as 無名，天地之始；有名，萬物之母, which means, "Nameless is the beginning of Heaven and Earth; named is the Mother of all things." But you can punctuate differently to read 無，名天地之始；有，名萬物之母. That way you get, "Nonbeing is the name of the beginning of Heaven and Earth; being is the name of the Mother of all things." Both readings make sense and both have existed throughout the history of *Daodejing* studies.

In addition to the above, there are three characters in this chapter that call for special attention. The first is 觀 (*guān*), meaning "to observe" or, in the case of internal meditation, "to contemplate." The Great Preface of *Yi Jing (I-Ching)* describes how the ancient sage Fuxi developed the immortal trigrams (prototypes of the hexagrams) by "observing" the patterns of the constellations up above in the sky and the patterns of the topography as well as the patterns of animal and plant behaviors down below on earth. Fully aware of the difficulty of articulating the "secrets" of the *Dao* in words, Laozi puts off his attempt to probe into that realm until a much later chapter. But he invites us to "observe" both the mystery and the manifestations of the *Dao*. To Laozi, there are two modes of observation, both of which are valid. One is to dispense with the human desire for sensuous gratification and focus on contemplating the "mystery" of Nonbeing. The other is to make good use of the human gift of intellectual curiosity and observe the all and sundry "manifestations" in the state of Being. Incidentally, it is interesting to note that in Daoist religion, a temple is not called a "temple" but an "observatory," using exactly the same character 觀.

Another key word in this chapter is the character 母 (*mǔ*) for "mother" in the phrase 萬物之母, "the Mother of all things." In a patriarchal society where the "father" is almost universally acknowledged as the originator of all beings, it is most enlightening to note the feminist propensity of the Daoist teachings in seeing the Mother as the ultimate Creator. Such an archetypal discernment is based on the close observation of the patterns of the universe and found in all the figures of speech that the Daoist philosophy adopts. One such lies in the word 玄 (*xuán*), meaning "dark" and by derivation "profound" or "mysterious." From Laozi's use of this word and related terms, that which is dark and thus leads to the far depth of the ultimate truth from which life exudes has definitely a sexual connotation as well as cosmic significance. For further elaboration see chapter 6.

Given the generally received order of chapters, Laozi is preparing his readers from the outset not just for another book of wisdom on the ways of the world but for something really big and profound, something all-inclusive and originative, something almost ineffable and intangible. At the same time he is promising his readers something observable and accessible—"the gateway to all mysteries," as long as they follow the right paths of access and modes of observation.

2

天下皆知美之为美，斯恶矣。皆知善之为善，斯不善矣。

有无相生、难易相成、长短相形、高下相倾、音声相和、前后相随：恒也。

是以圣人处无为之事，行不言之教；万物作而弗始，生而弗有，为而弗恃，功成而弗居。夫唯弗居，是以不去。

天下皆知美之爲美	When all under Heaven know beauty as beauty,
斯惡矣	There is ugliness.
皆知善之爲善	When all know good as good,
斯不善矣	There is the not good.

有無相生	Being and Nonbeing generate one another;
難易相成	Difficult and easy complement one another;
長短相形	Long and short give form to one another;
高下相傾	High and low depend on one another;
音聲相和	Music and voice harmonize one another;
前後相隨	Front and rear follow one another:
恒也	These are constant.

是以	That is why
聖人處無爲之事	The sage handles affairs by Non-doing (*wuwei*),
行不言之教	And practices teaching by not speaking.
萬物作而弗始	He lets all things happen but does not initiate,
生而弗有	Lets them grow but does not possess,
爲而弗恃	Gets things done but does not take advantage,
功成而弗居	Achieves his goal but claims no credit.
夫唯弗居	Just because he claims no credit,
是以不去	His credit does not go away.

COMMENTARY ....

In the first stanza Laozi is making a couple of statements that may sound contradictory or even absurd at first. But, upon closer examination, they turn out to be wise discernment of the truths in life. Such statements are paradoxes, and by invoking paradoxes Laozi teaches us how to transcend the differences forged by the human mind and be at peace with Nature's creations. For example, Nature or *Dao* created the "ten thousand things under Heaven" without making distinctions between the ugly and the beautiful, the good and the not good. It is only we humans who created such distinctions. It is we humans who crave for the beautiful and good and loathe the ugly and the not good. Such cravings and loathing lead to strife and agony, and that in itself is ugly and not good.

Following the two paradoxes about beauty and good versus ugliness and not good, Laozi posits one of mankind's first cracks at relativity—the interdependence of opposites such as Being versus Nonbeing, easy versus difficult, long versus short, and so on. "Music and voice," by the way, refers to instrumental and vocal music. Then, in one of Laozi's characteristic sequences, marked by his use of "therefore" and "thus" and "that is why," he teaches us how to follow the sage's behavior accordingly. Given the received order of the chapters, this is Laozi's first mention of his hero 聖人 (*shèng rén*) or "sage." To Laozi, the sage is not so much a moral exemplar as someone who is endowed with the wisdom to get things done without any arbitrary or self-serving action. Such a notion of wise "Non-doing" or "not doing," known as 無爲 (*wú wéi*), is going to become a leitmotif that runs throughout the pages of this book, but here the author seems to throw it out casually as if it was a familiar term, suggesting that he is probably not the first user of the expression. However, Laozi does go on to elaborate what he means by "Non-doing" or "not doing" and clinches the point by a guaranteed reward: "Just because he claims no credit, his credit does not go away." This closing sentence strongly suggests that Laozi's philosophy is not just about pure metaphysics or ethics but has the applicative value of gaining the desired result with the least effort.

A word may be said about "teaching without speaking" or "teaching without words." Posterity has ridiculed Laozi by citing his work of five thousand words as rebuttal to his own principle. While recognizing the ineffability of *Dao* as the sage implies, we need not take his words literally and attempt a total denial of the role of words in teaching.

3

··

不尚贤，使民不争；不贵难得之货，使民不盗；不见可欲，使民心不乱。

是以圣人之治，虚其心，实其腹、弱其志，强其骨。常使民无知无欲。使夫智者不敢为也。为无为，则无不治。

不尚賢	Do not glorify the talented
使民不爭	So the common people will not contend.
不貴難得之貨	Do not value rare goods
使民不盜	So the common people will not steal.
不見可欲	Do not display objects of desire
使民心不亂	So the common people's minds will not be confused.
是以聖人之治	Thus the sage through his governance
虛其心	Keeps their minds empty,
實其腹	Their bellies full,
弱其志	Their wills weak,
強其骨	Their bones strong.
常使民無知無欲	He always keeps his people away from knowledge and desire,
使夫智者不敢爲也	So that the knowledgeable ones do not dare to act.
爲無爲	Apply Non-doing
則無不治	And there is nothing that he cannot govern.

COMMENTARY ···

A word Laozi uses frequently when he discusses social issues is 民 (*mín*), the common people. The *min* in Laozi's time refers specifically to the silent, illiterate, benighted majority. They eked out an existence by the sweat of their brows, were forced to serve as corvée labor, and were conscripted to fight in war. When they were driven to desperation by tyranny or natural disaster, they would turn into rioting mobs and bring social unrest. Despite the universal value of Laozi's teachings, it would be ahistorical to expect Laozi to address *min* directly as his audience. To bring peace and well-being to society, he had to appeal to the sensibility of the rulers as well as the educated and privileged few to keep the common people at peace and under control. That was the historical reality he had to face. That does not mean he did not have the common people's well-being in mind when he gave counsel to the rulers.

It is in this context that Laozi advised against glorifying the talented, or 尚賢 (*shàng xián*), a term used by Mozi (c. 468–376 BCE), one of the most influential thinkers of the Warring States period. Mozi was advising the rulers to avoid judging people only by their social status but reward people for their talents and merits. Laozi opposed the idea because he thought such promotion would incite the common people to contend for higher positions. To Laozi, a sage ruler was one who knew how to keep his subjects' minds at peace and their bodies well fed. In an agrarian society plagued by centuries of war, to keep the people's bellies full and their bones strong was no easy job. Remember the Chinese saying "To the common people, food is the topmost priority." Remember also that in pre-industrial times, the bones and muscles were all the physical power that people had at their disposal to make a living with.

According to the Lord of the River (He Shang Gong), whose edition of *Laozi* with line-by-line commentaries dates back to the Eastern Han dynasty (25–220), a sage's governance is not just about politics and economy but also about the ruler's self-cultivation. Thus, to empty the mind could mean to "clear the mind of all desires and worries," to fill the belly could mean to "embrace *Dao* and protect one's spiritual essence," to weaken the will could mean to "maintain an attitude of humility and yielding and never crave for power," and to strengthen the bones could mean to "cherish one's vital energy and keep one's bones filled with marrows." All this points to the principle of Non-doing, by which there is nothing that cannot be governed.

4

....

道沖，而用之或不盈。渊兮，似万物之宗；湛兮，似或存。吾不知谁之子；
象帝之先。

道沖	*Dao* is an empty vessel,
而用之或不盈	It is used and never gets filled up:
渊兮似萬物之宗	Deep like the source of all things;
湛兮似或存	Dark and vaguely present.
吾不知誰之子	I do not know whose child it is;
象帝之先	Its manifestation precedes the Divine Ruler.

COMMENTARY ....

Laozi likens *Dao* to an empty vessel, 沖 being a variant character of 盅, meaning "vessel" and by extension the vacuity of a vessel. Based on an "emendation" of the character 盈 (*yíng*), meaning "full," to the character 窮 (*qióng*), meaning "exhausted" in an earlier redaction, one scholar translates the first two lines as: "The way is empty, yet use will not drain it." Both the emendator and translator may have in mind a cross reference to the lines "Great abundance seems empty; its use is inexhaustible" in chapter 45. But the usefulness of a vessel lies precisely in its inexhaustible "emptiness." You can use the vacuity of a vessel as long as you can pour liquid into it, but the capacity of *Dao* is such that it never gets used up. By choosing the word "drain" the translator shifts away from Laozi's fascination with the paradoxical usefulness of emptiness and lands in the mundane attachment to material abundance. That certainly goes against the grain of Laozi's perception of *Dao*.

The word 帝 (*di*) refers to the Heavenly Ruler, the highest being that rules the universe. Laozi says that *Di* is actually preceded by *Dao* and *Dao* is not birthed by anything else. By the way, it was not until the First Emperor of Qin (Qin Shi Huangdi) conquered China that the title *Di* began to take on the meaning of the human "emperor."

5

天地不仁，以万物为刍狗；圣人不仁，以百姓为刍狗。

天地之间，其犹橐龠乎？虚而不屈，动而愈出。

多言数穷；不如守中。

天地不仁	Heaven and Earth are not humane,
以萬物爲芻狗	They treat all things like straw dogs.
聖人不仁	The sage is not humane,
以百姓爲芻狗	He treats all people like straw dogs.
天地之間	The space between Heaven and Earth—
其猶橐籥乎	Isn't it like the bellows?
虛而不屈	Empty but never exhausted,
動而愈出	Dynamic and ever more productive.
多言數窮	Too many words lead to quick exhaustion;
不如守中	Better stay centered.

COMMENTARY

Much ink has been spilled trying to explain why Laozi thinks "the sage" as well as "Heaven and Earth" are not kind or humane. The consensus seems to be that when Laozi says, "不仁 (bù rén)," he does not really mean "not kind" or "not humane." Actually no such explanation is due. As we can see, the character 仁 (rén) is made up of two parts, the left radical meaning "human" and the right half meaning "two." It tells us that 仁 (rén) is a human concept and specifically involves relationships between two or more people. But Heaven and Earth, and *Dao* itself for that matter, stand far above such human concepts. Commentators from Wang Bi on down have rightly pointed out that Heaven and Earth do not act out of such anthropomorphic motivation as human kindness but just be and let Nature or *Dao* take care of everything. Some translators try to substitute "not kind" or "not humane" with "reject kin-kindness" or "ruthless" or "impartial," and the like. But these are also human concepts that have no business with Heaven and Earth. "Straw dogs" are sacrificial objects that are burned and discarded after serving their purpose. Users show no particular attachment to any of these objects. Heaven and Earth treat all things with no particular attachment, just as the sage treats his people with no particular attachment. Should Heaven and Earth or the sage become preoccupied with showing kindness or humanity, they lose their equilibrium. Laozi does not mince his words when he confronts the core Confucian value 仁 (*rén*) and calls it into question. We will examine further Laozi's challenges to Confucian values in later chapters. Suffice it to say for now that given his earlier questioning of the much used terms 道 (*dào*) and 名 (*míng*) in chapter 1, we have good reason to believe that Laozi's writing is in many ways a reaction to and a product of the polemics of the day. In other words, Laozi established his own school of thought that needed no disclaimers.

Laozi's argument about the non-human character of Heaven and Earth is reinforced by his metaphor of the bellows in the second half of the chapter. For the bellows to be an effective tool, it has to leave the airway at its center clear. Moreover, this empty space has to maintain its open-and-shut dynamic so that the bellows can remain productive as it is required. This is exactly what we find in the vast space between Heaven and Earth. If Heaven and Earth should start acting and stop being, they would lose their centeredness and their balanced rhythm. Without this centered vibrancy, Heaven and Earth would lose the vital energy (*Qi*) to support the myriad things. By the same token, if the ruler should obsess himself with exercising benevolent rule and issuing too many decrees, he would soon lose his equilibrium. That is why Laozi says, "Too many words lead to quick exhaustion; better stay centered." By that Laozi does not mean staying with "the mean," which is a Confucian concept, but staying within the empty space.

6

谷神不死；是谓玄牝。玄牝之门，是谓天地根。绵绵若存，用之不勤。

谷神不死	The spirit of the valley never dies;
是謂玄牝	It is called the profound female.
玄牝之門	The gateway of the profound female
是謂天地根	Is called the root of Heaven and Earth.
縣縣若存	Continuously it seems to last,
用之不勤	Useful but never overworked.

COMMENTARY

For the first time in the present order of *Daodejing*, Laozi invokes the "spirit of the valley" and equates it with the profound female. Like the empty vessel in chapter 4, the valley remains vacuous and never gets filled to the brim—a great symbol of humble service. Laozi is fascinated by the infinite capacity of the deep, the dark, the empty, the concave. He observes this capacity in the empty vessel, the center of the bellows, the "spirit" of the valley, and, above all else, the mysterious depth of the female organs. The mention of the last item is particularly significant because unlike the prudish Confucius who shies away from any subject involving sex, Laozi has no qualms addressing whatever Nature has to offer for his contemplation. His analogy of female anatomy, reflecting his profound respect for the female, is closely embedded in his perception of *Dao* as the **Mother** of all things. We will see more analogies of the valley as well as the female organs as we progress.

7

....

天长地久。天地所以能长且久者，以其不自生。故能长生。

是以圣人后其身而身先；外其身而身存。非以其无私邪？故能成其私。

天長地久	Heaven lives long and Earth is lasting.
天地所以能長且久者	The reason why Heaven and Earth are long-lasting
以其不自生	Is that they do not will their own existence.
故能長生	That is why they live long.
是以	Thus,
聖人後其身而身先	The sage puts himself in the rear and yet ends up in front;
外其身而身存	He places himself on the outside and yet remains present.
非以其無私邪	Isn't it because he is selfless
故能成其私	That he is able to fulfill himself?

COMMENTARY ....

Heaven and Earth do not will their existence. They do not try to make their long-lasting existence happen; they just be. The result is that they not only exist but also exist for long. The sage follows Heaven and Earth as his role model by refusing to push himself in front of everyone else. But by yielding he earns people's respect and ends up ahead of everyone else. By the same token, because he does not pursue his self-interest, he finds himself well fulfilled. Laozi is not advocating a self-promoting ruse so much as pointing out a paradox which is one of the secrets of *Dao*, the way things are.

8

上善若水。水善利万物而不争，处众人之所恶，故几于道。

居善地，心善渊，与善仁，言善信，政善治，事善能，动善时。

夫唯不争。故无尤。

上善若水	The highest good is like water:
水善利萬物而不爭	Water brings good to all things and does not contend;
處眾人之所惡	It goes to places which most people detest
故幾於道	And is therefore akin to *Dao*.
居善地	Dwell on good ground;
心善淵	Meditate in good depth;
與善仁	Keep good company;
言善信	Speak in good faith;
政善治	Rule with good policy;
事善能	Serve with good competence;
動善時	Act with good timing.
夫唯不爭	Because there is no contention.
故無尤	There is no blame.

COMMENTARY

Laozi sees water as the quintessential embodiment of good. In water he sees humility and non-contention. He repeats the word "good" or 善 (*shàn*) over and over again: twice in the opening two lines and then seven times, each at the center of a three-character line in the third stanza. This repetition often gets lost in translation, but I try to keep it along with the parallel structures so that my English readers can get a sense of the power of Laozi's poetic language. Laozi uses the word "good" not only in the sense of moral excellence but effective competence. From Laozi's point of view, the two are complementary. Being morally good but incapable of accomplishing anything amounts to "good for nothing." On the other hand, being effective in all one's dealings but lacking a good heart to begin with is fundamentally flawed.

The importance Laozi attaches to water, claiming it to be "akin to *Dao*," is no accident. Like the valley, it is one of the most poignant symbols of humility. This is corroborated by the Guodian text, 太一生水 (*Tài Yī Shēng Shuǐ*), "The Great One Gives Birth to Water." This newly discovered text on bamboo strips, bound together with a script of *Daodejing*, begins with the sentence, "The Great One Gives Birth to Water, and Water, in its turn, assists the Great One."

9

持而盈之，不如其已；揣而锐之，不可长保。金玉满堂，莫之能守；富贵而骄，自遗其咎。功遂身退，天之道也。

持而盈之	Holding a cup while filling it to the brim
不如其已	Is not as good as stopping then and there.
揣而锐之	Hammering the blade till it is sharp
不可長保	Cannot keep it so for long.
金玉滿堂	Stuffing the hall with gold and jade
莫之能守	Does not guarantee it will stay secure.
富貴而驕	Turning arrogant after gaining wealth and position
自遺其咎	Brings disaster upon oneself.
功遂身退	Retire after achieving one's goal—
天之道也	That is the *Dao* of Heaven.

COMMENTARY ....

In contrast to the humility of water, Laozi sees a pattern of insatiable desires among his fellow beings, especially the rich and powerful. Yet such pursuits for wealth and power inevitably lead to pride and fall. Instead of continuing on this disastrous path, his advice is to quit at the height of success. He draws a series of images from everyday life, such as keeping on filling a cup while holding it, keeping on hammering a blade hoping it will stay sharp forever, filling one's hall with gold and jade hoping the hoarding will stay secure, and so on, to illustrate the human tendency to overreach oneself. He hammers home his point with the last two lines: "Retire after achieving one's goal—That is the *Dao* of Heaven."

It is interesting that Laozi uses the term "the *Dao* of Heaven" as an equivalent of "the eternal *Dao*." Heaven or 天 (*ti'n*) is widely accepted throughout Chinese history as the supreme being of the universe, but, as Laozi points out, it is preceded by *Dao* and has to follow the ways of *Dao*.

10

....

载营魄抱一，能无离乎？专气致柔，能如婴儿乎？涤除玄鉴，能无疵乎？爱民治国，能无为乎？天门开阖，能为雌乎？明白四达，能无知乎？

載營魄抱一	Embracing the One with both your spirit and soul,
能無離乎	Can you stay seamless?
專氣致柔	Focusing your *Qi* till you reach suppleness,
能如嬰兒乎	Can you be like an infant?
滌除玄鑒	Wiping your Mystery Mirror clean,
能無疵乎	Can you make sure it remains unblemished?
愛民治國	Caring for your people and governing your state,
能無爲乎	Can you apply Non-doing?
天門開闔	Letting your portals open and shut,
能爲雌乎	Can you maintain your femininity?
明白四達	Keeping all four directions free and clear,
能無知乎	Can you remain unknowing?

COMMENTARY ....

Laozi asks a series of questions all ending with the question marker 乎 (*hū*). The first three questions have to do with building the spiritual foundation; the next three seem more concerned with application.

Ancient Chinese believed that every human being has two souls, 魂 (*hùn*) (here 營 *yíng*) and 魄 (*pò*). The former, which I translate as "spirit," can exist independently from the body, whereas the latter, which I translate as "soul," stays with the body. Together they make life whole and keep it connected with the One—the greater, inexhaustible *Qi* or vital energy emanating from *Dao*. How can this lifeline be maintained? By "focusing your *Qi* till you reach suppleness" "like an infant." As the pseudonymic Lord of the River puts it in his commentary, "If you focus on your essential *Qi* and protect it from disruptions, your body will respond and become soft and supple."

A word about the character *Qi*. In modern Chinese writing, it is 气 in the simplified syllabary and 氣 in the traditional or "complicated" syllabary. But in ancient texts, such as in the Han dynasty dictionary *Shuo Wen Jie Zi*, both forms coexist. It means "air" or "breath" in the physical sense of the word and "life force" or "vital energy" in the vocabulary of spiritual cultivators. The "complicated" 氣 refers specifically to the vital energy or nutrition drawn from food as symbolized by the component 米 (*mǐ*) for "rice" or "grain." The "simplified" 气 refers specifically to the life-sustaining force that comes from breath or air, which is invisible as a character component. Laozi may have had both forms of *Qi* in mind when he speaks of the special gift of the infant.

The infant is the purest, the most tranquil and most potent being on earth. If we can maintain the innocence of our infancy, we should have no problem maintaining our connectedness with *Dao*, which is the ultimate source of our vital energy. Again, as the Lord of the River says, "If, like the infant, you can be free from thoughts and worries on the inside and state affairs and business dealings on the outside, your essence and spirit will not go away."

"Mystery Mirror" is a literal translation for the mirror through which one can see far into the profound mystery of *Dao* and deep into one's inner self at the same time. This mirror is none other than one's inner vision, "the eye within," as Moss Roberts (2004, 48) puts it. To maintain its lucidity, one has to wipe it constantly and keep it clear of all stray thoughts and illusions.

Keeping to the One, focusing the *Qi*, keeping the inner vision clear—all these require intensive self-cultivation and concentrated meditation. But they are necessary steps toward understanding the secrets of *Dao*.

"Caring for the people and governing the state" normally demands a good deal of action and effort on the part of the ruler. But Laozi is challenging the ruler to do all this without any conscious effort, even without doing. This is the third time Laozi invokes the principle of Non-doing or 無爲 (*wú wéi*). To Laozi, the question is not whether it can be done but how. There are more occasions where he develops this idea.

The Heavenly Portal or 天門 (*tiān mén*), in the singular, refers to the spot at the center of the forehead. It is also known as the Third Eye. In the plural, it may refer, according to the Lord of the River, to the nostrils through which one breathes, or, according to later commentators, the sensory organs or portals, including the eyes, ears, nose, and mouth. Since Chinese nouns have no morphological indicator for number, I just adopt the simpler and more general "portals." Most human beings busy themselves opening and shutting their portals to satisfy their sensuous desires so their minds are never at peace. That is a masculine way of life. Laozi is asking for an alternative, feminine way of life whereby one still needs to open and shut their portals but can do it in a peaceful way. That is what he means by maintaining one's femininity. Remember Laozi tells us from the beginning that *Dao* is the "Mother of all things" and that the root of Heaven and Earth is the "mysterious female."

Remaining unknowing means refusing to have one's mind clogged with mundane information. Only this way can you keep your mind free and clear in all directions.

11

三十辐共一毂：当其无，有车之用。

埏埴以为器：当其无，有器之用。

凿户牖以为室：当其无，有室之用。

故有之以为利，无之以为用。

三十輻共一轂	Thirty spokes converge at the hub:
當其無	Where there is nothing
有車之用	There lies what makes the cart useful.
埏埴以爲器	Mix clay to make a vessel:
當其無	Where there is nothing
有器之用	There lies what makes the vessel useful.
鑿戶牖以爲室	Chisel doors and windows to make a house:
當其無	Where there is nothing
有室之用	There lies what makes the house useful.
故有之以爲利	Thus things bring benefits;
無之以爲用	Nothingness brings usefulness.

COMMENTARY

An oxcart or carriage with thirty spokes to each wheel—that must be a huge vehicle. But one must not forget the spokes would be of no use and the cart worthless if there wasn't the empty space at the center of the hub. The same is true of a utensil. You can make a beautiful pottery vessel and brag about it. But what makes the vessel useful is the empty space within. The same is also true of a house. Despite the builder's exquisite woodwork, it is the empty space within and the hollows of the doors and windows that let in the fresh air and make the house useful. So, after illustrating the unfathomable depth of *Dao* as symbolized by the empty space of the valley, the vessel, the womb, and anything else that is concave, Laozi is reminding us of the practical value of empty space in everyday objects. In doing so, he is directing our attention away from the tangible material substance to the intangible but far more meaningful space in and around us. Notice the repetition of the word 無 (*wú*) for "nothing" or "nothingness" echoing the same repetition in chapter 1.

12

五色令人目盲；五音令人耳聾；五味令人口爽；馳騁畋猎，令人心发狂；难得之货，令人行妨。

是以圣人为腹不为目。故去彼取此。

五色令人目盲	The five colors dazzle one's eyes;
五音令人耳聾	The five sounds deafen one's ears;
五味令人口爽	The five flavors numb one's palate.
馳騁畋獵	Galloping and hunting
令人心發狂	Turn one's mind loose;
難得之貨	Goods hard to come by
令人行妨	Turn one's conduct awry.
是以	That is why
聖人爲腹不爲目	The sage focuses on the belly, not the eye.
故去彼取此	Hence he disregards the latter and adopts the former.

COMMENTARY

The five colors are blue, red, yellow, white, and black. The five sounds correspond to the pentatonic scale. The five flavors are sour, bitter, sweet, spicy, and salty. But "five" in Chinese can also be an approximate number signifying multiplicity. So it is possible to translate the first three lines without literally rendering the "five." In fact the English might read even better without impairing the meaning.

The belly may mean the stomach that you feed regularly with food, but in Daoist terms it also refers to the lower abdomen called *dantian* where *Qi* or vital energy is stored. It is the center of spiritual cultivation. In chapter 3 "fill the belly" could mean "fill it both with *Qi* and with food," but in the context of this chapter the sage does not seem to take food as his top priority.

....

13

宠辱若惊，贵大患若身。

何谓宠辱若惊？宠为下，得之若惊，失之若惊，是谓宠辱若惊。

何谓贵大患若身？吾所以有大患者，为吾有身，及吾无身，吾有何患？

故贵以身为天下，若可寄天下；爱以身为天下，若可托天下。

| 寵辱若驚 | Favor is as alarming as disfavor; |
| 貴大患若身 | Caring about disaster is like caring about oneself. |

何謂寵辱若驚	Why say, "Favor is as alarming as disfavor"?
寵爲下	Favor is no good;
得之若驚	Gaining it is alarming;
失之若驚	Losing it is alarming;
是謂寵辱若驚	Hence, "Favor is as alarming as disfavor."

何謂貴大患若身	Why say, "Caring about disaster is like caring about oneself"?
吾所以有大患者	The reason why I have disaster
爲吾有身	Is because I have a self.
及吾無身	If I don't have a self,
吾有何患	What disaster do I have?

故	Therefore,
貴以身爲天下	If you care about yourself for the sake of the world,
若可寄天下	You may be charged with the world;
愛以身爲天下	If you love yourself for the sake of the world,
若可託天下	You may be entrusted with the world.

COMMENTARY

"Favor is as alarming as disfavor." Nobody wants to fall into disfavor. That is taken for granted. But what about favor? In a feudal state, almost everyone wants to curry favor with the ruler. But once you become his favorite, you fall under his absolute control and could easily forfeit his favor with dire consequences even through no fault of your own. That is why Laozi makes the argument that favor is just as alarming as disfavor.

"Caring about disaster is like caring about oneself." It may not be difficult for us to agree that we are afraid of disasters because we all have a self. If we have no self, we need fear no disaster because there is no disaster to speak of. The logical conclusion would be, then, "Just give up your self, your self-love, and self-interest and there will be no disaster." But Laozi turns this line of thinking around by pointing out that only if you care about yourself would you take disasters seriously. In fact, your self-love can be a great asset as a potential leader. For if you know how to take care of yourself and prevent disaster, you will qualify to lead the world through trials and tribulations. Laozi was not a high-sounding moralist preaching selflessness or self-sacrifice and denying the worth of self-interest. He was very down to earth when it comes to solving the dilemmas of the human condition.

14

视之不见，名曰夷；听之不闻，名曰希；抟之不得，名曰微。此三者不可致诘，故混而为一。

其上不皦；其下不昧。绳绳兮不可名，复归于无物。是谓无状之状，无物之象，是谓惚恍。迎之不见其首，随之不见其后。

执古之道，以御今之有。能知古始，是谓道纪。

視之不見名曰夷	That which one can look at but not see is called *Yi*;
聽之不聞名曰希	That which one can listen to but not hear is called *Xi*;
搏之不得名曰微	That which one can grapple for but not grasp is called *Wei*.
此三者不可致詰	These three defy close inquiry,
故混而爲一	And are therefore lumped together as One.
其上不皦	Its top is not bright;
其下不昧	Its bottom is not dark.
繩繩兮不可名	Lush and lasting but unnamable,
復歸於無物	It returns to a state of nothingness.
是謂無狀之狀	This is called form without form,
無物之象	And image of nothingness,
是謂惚恍	Known as "evasive."
迎之不見其首	From the front you don't see its head,
隨之不見其後	From the back you don't see its rear.
執古之道	Applying the *Dao* of ancient times
以御今之有	To harness the things of today
能知古始	Enables us to understand the ancient beginnings—
是謂道紀	That is called the lineage of *Dao*.

COMMENTARY ....

Laozi uses three interesting words, 夷 (*Yí*) (invisibility), 希 (*Xī*) (inaudibility), and 微 (*Wēi*) (intangibility), to define the attributes of *Dao*. He adds that these three "defy close inquiry" and therefore have to be blended together and called "One." To honor this shroud of mystery, I just transliterate the pronunciation of the three Chinese characters without translating them.

The "evasive" nature of *Dao* is described further in the next stanza. If we see an object coming our way, we would normally see its top catching the light and its bottom hidden in the shadow. But in the case of the One, we see neither. In fact, it does not even have a form. That is why we don't see its head from the front or its rear from the back. What Laozi is talking about is not the legendary "invisible man" but a "nothingness," a form without form.

It is interesting that Laozi makes no mention of the word *Dao* in the first two stanzas but names it twice in the short concluding stanza. He thinks it is imperative to apprehend the complex reality of today in the light of its ancient origin. He calls this connectedness between past and present "the lineage of *Dao*."

15

古之善为士者，微妙玄通，深不可识。夫唯不可识，故强为之容：

豫兮若冬涉川；犹兮若畏四邻；俨兮其若客；涣兮其若凌释；敦兮其若朴；旷兮其若谷；混兮其若浊；澹兮其若海；飚兮若无止。

孰能浊以静之徐清？孰能安以动之徐生？

保此道者，不欲盈。夫唯不盈，故能蔽而新成。

古之善爲士者	Well-cultivated men of ancient times
微妙玄通	Had a profound understanding of the mysterious,
深不可識	Too deep to comprehend.
夫唯不可識	Just because they cannot be comprehended,
故强爲之容	I do my best to describe their demeanor:
豫兮若冬涉川	Gingerly as if wading across a winter river;
猶兮若畏四鄰	Wary as if fearful of the neighbors;
儼兮其若客	Formal like a guest;
涣兮其若凌釋	Melting like the thaw;
敦兮其若樸	Ingenuous like raw timber;
曠兮其若谷	Open like the valley;
混兮其若濁	Natural like muddy water;
澹兮其若海	Calm like the sea;
飂兮若無止	Airy like the unceasing wind.
孰能濁以静之徐清	Who could calm the muddy till it slowly clears?
孰能安以動之徐生	Who could stir the quiet till it slowly revives?

保此道者不欲盈	Those who practice this *Dao* do not seek fullness.
夫唯不盈	Because they do not seek fullness
故能蔽而新成	They can always rejuvenate themselves.

COMMENTARY

Since *Dao* itself is intangible and evasive, as Laozi has explained in the previous chapter, he turns to another approach by looking for clues in the typical demeanor of a *Dao* seeker. Here he invokes the term 士 (*shi*), which in his time was used to refer to a special class of well-educated people who were superior in social status to 民 (*mín*), the common people. To quote the famous definition of *shi* by Confucius, "A person who studies and excels is a *shi* [scholar]." Laozi seems to hold higher standards for the *shi* as he says the *shi* of ancient times had profound understanding of the mysterious.

Incidentally there is a subtle point of textual difference here that may interest the readers. According to the received version, the first line of this chapter reads, "古之善爲士者 (*gǔ zhī shàn wéi shì zhě*)" (those who excel as scholars in ancient times). But according to the Mawangdui silk scripts, the same line reads, "古之善爲道者 (*gǔ zhī shàn wéi dào zhě*)" (those who excel in *Dao* in ancient times). Assuming the Mawangdui version predates the received version, some of the more recent translators switched from *shi* to *Dao*. But with the discovery of the Guodian bamboo script, which dates even earlier than Mawangdui and which reaffirms the use of *shi* instead of *Dao*, the *shi* version won the day.

To give the readers a description of the characteristic behavior of a *Dao*-cultivating scholar, Laozi proceeds to depict a series of vivid images in the second stanza. By these images one can visualize a person who is extremely cautious and humble, ingenuous and natural, open and gentle. In case you wonder if such a character is capable of wielding any power, Laozi throws in a couplet after the long stanza to indicate that the ancient master indeed had the power to clear the murky and reactivate the still, exactly the kind of power a ruler needs in unstable times. How could a person with such humility have such power? The answer comes in the last stanza, where Laozi reinvokes the quality of "not seeking fullness" or 不盈 (*bù yíng*), which he mentions in chapter 4, where he compares *Dao* to an empty vessel that never overfills.

16

致虚极，守静笃。万物并作，吾以观复。

夫物芸芸，各复归其根。归根曰静，静曰复命；复命曰常，知常曰明。不知常，妄作凶。

知常容，容乃公；公乃全，全乃天，天乃道，道乃久，没身不殆。

致虛極	Push emptiness to the limit;
守靜篤	Keep still to the extreme;
萬物並作	All things thrive;
吾以觀復	I observe their return.
夫物芸芸	For when things grow profuse,
各復歸其根	They return to their respective roots.
歸根曰靜	Return to the roots is called tranquility;
靜曰復命	Tranquility is called regaining one's nature;
復命曰常	Regaining one's nature is called constancy;
知常曰明	Knowing the constant is called wisdom.
不知常	Not knowing the constant
妄作凶	Leads to disastrous acts of violence.
知常容	Knowing the constant leads to acceptance;
容乃公	Acceptance means impartiality;
公乃全	Impartiality means inclusiveness;
全乃天	Inclusiveness means the way of Heaven;
天乃道	The way of Heaven means *Dao*;
道乃久	*Dao* means eternity;
沒身不殆	To the end of your life you will have no peril.

COMMENTARY ....

The first stanza invites the readers to enter a state of absolute tranquility and observe the patterns of behavior of all things in Nature. The key word here is again 觀 (*guān*), "to observe" or "to contemplate," in the sense as it is used in chapter 1. The first-person "I" (吾 *wú*) does not have to be Laozi himself. It could be anybody in the process of contemplation. As he observes the life cycle of all things, what he sees is a pattern of return to the roots. Only when things return to their roots can they find the tranquil source of vital energy to renew themselves. Laozi considers this cycle of birth, growth, return, and renewal "constant" because it is a recurrent, invariable pattern that reflects the way of Heaven or the law of *Dao*. Once you are attuned to this constant cycle, your mind becomes receptive, impartial, and open to all. In this way you eventually reach *Dao* and enjoy longevity.

Note the repeated sentence patterns "A is called B; B is called C," and so on, and "A means B, B means C," and so on, which reflect the recurrent cycle of all things in Nature. It is typical of Laozi's vigorous prose style, which is as compelling as his poetry.

17

太上，不知有之；其次，亲而誉之；其次，畏之；其次，侮之。信不足焉，有
不信焉。

悠兮其贵言。功成事遂，百姓皆谓：我自然。

太上不知有之	The best ruler is one whose presence is unknown;
其次親而譽之	The second best is one who is beloved and praised;
其次畏之	The next best is one who is feared;
其次侮之	The next is one who is despised.
信不足焉	Where there is insufficient good faith,
有不信焉	There is loss of faith.
悠兮其貴言	Relax and spare your words.
功成事遂	When the goal is achieved and the job is done,
百姓皆謂	Everyone says,
我自然	"We did it."

COMMENTARY

The reason why so many aspirant rulers end up being despised is because they take on too much or make too many promises. The last two lines of the first stanza make the point by playing on the word 信 (*xìn*). This character is made up of two parts: the left radical 人 (*rén*) stands for "human" and the right half 言 (*yán*) means words, that is, verbal statements, be they promises or instructions. The two parts put together make the character 信, meaning truthfulness, good faith, belief, and so on. It suggests that the words uttered by a human being should be sincere and therefore trustworthy. Thus the 信 in the first of the two lines means "credibility" or "good faith" and the 信 in the second line means "belief" or "faith." If the ruler makes too many promises and never keeps his word, the people lose their faith in him. That's the worst scenario. On the other hand, if he does not say much but lets the people do their job, people celebrate their own creativity and all but forget the ruler's presence. That, to Laozi, is the ideal ruler because he is one who rules by "doing nothing." To Laozi, a beloved and much eulogized leader is only second best, let alone one who rules by coercion or empty promises.

The characters 自然 (*zi rán*) in modern Chinese are used as one word meaning "Nature" or "natural." However, this meaning is derived from each of the two characters standing as an independent word, 自 (*zi*), meaning "self," and 然 (*rán*), meaning "like this" or "so." So the last line means "We ourselves made it so." For further explication of the meaning of 自然 (*zi rán*), see the commentary on chapter 25.

18

大道废，有仁义；慧智出，有大伪；六亲不和，有孝慈；国家昏乱，有忠臣。

大道廢	When the great *Dao* is abandoned,
有仁義	There is humankindness and righteousness.
慧智出	When wisdom and intelligence are put forth,
有大偽	There is outrageous falsehood.
六親不和	When the six relations are in disharmony,
有孝慈	There is filial piety and parental love.
國家昏亂	When the state is in disarray,
有忠臣	There appear loyal ministers.

COMMENTARY

This is one of the shortest and most poignant chapters in *Daodejing*. Here Laozi is posing a direct challenge to his contemporary Confucius on the latter's approach to social problems. Confucius promotes such ethical values as humankindness and righteousness, filial piety and parental love, loyalty and obedience as the proper remedies to social ills. But Laozi sees these much touted values as mere symptoms of the ills they are supposed to cure. He thinks the root of the problem lies not so much in not abiding by these artificial values as in the abandonment of the great *Dao*. If everyone embraced the *Dao*, there would be no need to promote those ethical doctrines. Laozi says in chapter 5, "Heaven and Earth are not humane," and "The sage is not humane." Those are his candid statements on the centerpiece of Confucian ethics, 仁 (*rén*), meaning "humankindness" or "humanity" or "benevolence."

It is important to remember that most commentators of *Daodejing* lived in the age when Confucian ethics had been canonized as the orthodoxy such that they would almost take the precepts of humankindness, righteousness, filial piety, loyalty, and so on for granted. This collective consciousness leads people to be on the defensive every time they see Confucian values being questioned by Laozi. This mentality may lurk behind some of the commentaries and textual preferences even to this day. A case in point lies in a recent explanation of the absence of the sentence "When wisdom and intelligence are put forth, there is outrageous falsehood" in the Guodian bamboo script. As the earliest extant script of *Daodejing*, Guodian understandably carries a good deal of weight when editorial decisions have to be made. But, when Chen Guying adopts the Guodian version, he argues that keeping the expunged sentence as is in the received version and the Mawangdui silk script might associate "humankindness and righteousness" in the previous line with "outrageous falsehood," thereby unjustly denigrating these indisputable ethical values. According to Chen, "humankindness and righteousness, filial piety and parental love, loyalty and obedience" are the best alternatives when society deviates from the pristine euphoric state and when social relations were in disarray (Chen 2009, 132). Chen's argument is a good example of the still prevailing resistance to Laozi's counter discourse. That said, Chen's adoption of the Guodian version does have a point. Minus the sentence about "outrageous falsehood," the Guodian chapter consists of three parallel structures, all following the pattern, "When Plan A fails, there is Plan B." The sentence about "falsehood," if restored, could be out of sync. We keep it because of its paradoxical content, which is in sync with the rest of the chapter.

Note: "The six relations" refers to father and son, older brother and younger brother, husband and wife—clearly a Confucian term for its patriarchal overtone.

19

绝圣弃智，民利百倍；绝仁弃义，民复孝慈。绝巧弃利，盗贼无有。此三者以为文，不足。故令有所属：见素抱朴，少私寡欲。

絕聖棄智	Reject sageness and discard knowledge,
民利百倍	And the common people will benefit hundreds of times.
絕仁棄義	Reject humankindness and discard righteousness,
民復孝慈	And the common people will restore familial love.
絕巧棄利	Reject smartness and discard profiteering,
盜賊無有	And thieves and robbers will disappear.
此三者以爲文不足	These three are inadequate as mere embellishments.
故令有所屬	Therefore we should tie them to their roots:
見素抱樸	Stay with the plain silk and embrace the pristine timber;
少私寡欲	Reduce selfishness and abstain from desires.

COMMENTARY

This chapter is an emphatic confirmation of Laozi's argument in the previous chapter. But the irony of Laozi's paradoxical statements is complicated by the discrepancy between the received version and the more recently discovered but chronologically earlier Guodian bamboo scripts. For "Reject sageness and discard knowledge" (絕聖棄智, *jué shèng qì zhì*), Guodian has "Reject cleverness and discard sophistry" (絕智棄辯, *jué zhì qì biàn*), and for "Reject humankindness and discard righteousness" (絕仁棄義, *jué rén qì yì*), Guodian has "Reject falsehood and discard deceit" (絕偽棄詐, *jué wěi qì zhà*). Again the age of the text is on the side of those who prefer the Guodian version, but in turning away from the received version, they resort to the same old argument: "How could Laozi have rejected humankindness and righteousness?" They especially seize upon the word "sageness" or 聖 (*shèng*), which Laozi uses "thirty-two times throughout the book in the expression 聖人 (the sage) in a positive sense" (Chen 2009, 134). How could Laozi ever reject sageness? But if we follow Laozi's consistent philosophy and rhetoric, this is really not hard to explain. The ancient sage in Laozi's language is one who practices *Dao* and lives in humility. He prefers the lowliest place and stays behind everybody else but ends up in front. He does not crave to be a sage but ends up being honored as one. It is precisely the craving for sageness that Laozi is rejecting.

20

绝学无忧。

唯之与阿，相去几何？美之与恶，相去若何？人之所畏，亦不可以不畏人。

荒兮其未央哉。众人熙熙，如享太牢，如春登台。我独泊兮，其未兆，沌沌兮如婴儿之未孩；儽儽兮，若无所归。众人皆有余，而我独若遗。我愚人之心也哉！俗人昭昭，我独昏昏。俗人察察，我独闷闷。众人皆有以，而我独顽且鄙。我独异于人，而贵食母。

絕學無憂	Give up studies and you will have no more worries.
唯之與阿	"Yes, sir?" and "Eh?"—
相去幾何	How far apart are these?
美之與惡	Beauty and ugliness—
相去若何	How different are those?
人之所畏	Whoever people fear
亦不可以不畏人	Has to fear the people too.

荒兮其未央哉	Vast and boundless,
眾人熙熙	Everyone is out having a great time,
如享太牢	As if enjoying a great feast,
如春登臺	As if climbing a terrace in spring.
我獨泊兮其未兆	I alone stay quiet and show no sign of action,
沌沌兮如嬰兒之未孩	Innocent like the unsmiling baby,
儽儽兮若無所歸	Wandering like not knowing where to go.
眾人皆有餘	Everyone has enough to spare;
而我獨若遺	I alone seem deprived.
我愚人之心也哉	It all has to do with my fool's heart!
俗人昭昭	The world thinks everything is crystal clear;

我獨昏昏	I alone am dull and dumb.
俗人察察	The world thinks they are sharp and shrewd;
我獨悶悶	I alone am simple and slow.
眾人皆有以	Everyone has something useful to do;
而我獨頑且鄙	I alone am incorrigibly stupid.
我獨異於人	I alone am different from everyone else
而貴食母	And choose to be nurtured by my mother.

COMMENTARY ···

The first line stands apart from the rest of the chapter. Some redactions treat it as a misplacement and move it to the end of the last chapter. We keep it here as a one-line synopsis of the entire chapter.

The line that says "Yes, sir?" and "Eh?" appears quite abrupt for its incongruous colloquialism. Actually Laozi is juxtaposing two everyday expressions used to respond to someone's calls. If that someone is somebody or your superior, you have to use the polite "唯 (wéi)," corresponding roughly to "Yes, sir?" If that person is someone who doesn't mind a casual reply, then you might just say, "阿 (ē)," something like "Eh?" In a society overly sensitive about rituals and propriety, the two responses make a world of difference. But from the perspective of *Dao*, does it matter if you are addressed politely or casually? Also what difference does it make if one sees something as beautiful and another as ugly? Then everyone, ruler and commoner alike, has to live with someone or something to fear. Incidentally I am using the Mawangdui version of these two lines. The received version alters the meaning by saying, "Whatever people fear, you have to fear too (人之所畏,不可不畏)." In any case, roaming free and aloof in this boundless universe, you just cannot care less about these inhibitions. With this mental state, you look at the mundane world around you and see everybody having a good time, celebrating what they possess or what they engage in, feeling complacent about their cleverness, yet you feel content with your dispassion, your aloofness, your seeming stupidity, and above all your singularity from everyone else. That is because you know you are connected with and nurtured by the Mother of all things, the ultimate source of vital energy—*Dao*.

Laozi repeatedly uses the first person 我 (*wǒ*) or "I" in contrast with the 衆人 (*zhòng rén*) (the multitude or everyone) or 俗人 (*sú rén*) (the worldlings or the worldly people). The "I" could be Laozi himself or a Daoist sage in general. He uses doublets for vividness, such as 昭昭 (*zhāo zhāo*) (crystal clear), 昏昏 (*hūn hūn*) (dull and dumb), 察察 (*chá chá*) (sharp and shrewd), and 悶悶 (*mēn mēn*) (simple and slow), a device that simply cannot be duplicated in translation except by my feeble attempts at alliteration.

21

孔德之容，惟道是从。

道之为物，惟恍惟惚。惚兮恍兮，其中有象；恍兮惚兮，其中有物。窈兮冥兮，其中有精；其精甚真，其中有信。

自今及古，其名不去。以阅众甫。吾何以知众甫之状哉？以此。

| 孔德之容 | The behavior of the Great *De* |
| 惟道是從 | Follows that of *Dao* and *Dao* alone. |

道之爲物	As a thing, *Dao* is
惟恍惟惚	Elusive and intangible.
惚兮恍兮	Intangible and elusive,
其中有象	Yet it contains the Image;
恍兮惚兮	Elusive and intangible,
其中有物	Yet it contains the thing.
窈兮冥兮	Dim and dark,
其中有精	Yet it contains the essence;
其精甚真	The essence is real,
其中有信	For it contains the truth.

自今及古	From the present back to antiquity,
其名不去	The name never disappears.
以閱衆甫	Through it I observe the beginning of all things.
吾何以知衆甫之狀哉	How do I know how all things began?
以此	Because of this.

COMMENTARY ....

If we read the chapters of *Daodejing* in the current order, this is the first time Laozi invokes the word *De* (德), a key concept, second only to that of *Dao*, in his school of thought. A fuller discussion of *De* will come later, but here he throws in two important clues to prepare his readers. First, he makes it clear that what he is talking about is the Great *De*, not the lesser *De* or virtues that the current usage of the word is associated with. Second, *De* as the emanation of *Dao* follows the behavior of *Dao* and *Dao* alone. So, as we can see in the second stanza, the chapter is more about *Dao* than *De*.

Different redactions of the received version all say, "From antiquity to the present," but we follow the Mawangdui scripts that say, "From the present back to antiquity." That is how we trace things to their historical origins.

22

曲则全、枉则直、洼则盈、敝则新、少则多，多则惑。

是以圣人抱一为天下式。不自见，故明；不自是，故彰；不自伐，故有功；不自矜，故长。

夫唯不争，故天下莫能与之争。古之所谓曲则全者，岂虚言哉。诚全而归之。

曲则全	Warped therefore intact;
枉则直	Bent therefore straight;
窪则盈	Hollowed therefore abundant;
敝则新	Used therefore renewed;
少则多	Little therefore much;
多则惑	Too much therefore befuddled.
是以	That is why
聖人抱一	The sage, adhering to the One,
爲天下式	Is a model to the world.
不自見	He does not exhibit himself
故明	And is therefore apparent;
不自是	He does not justify himself
故彰	And is therefore self-evident;
不自伐	He does not brag
故有功	And therefore earns credit;
不自矜	He is not arrogant
故長	And therefore lasts long.
夫唯不爭	Just because he does not contend,
故天下莫能与之爭	So the world cannot contend with him.
古之所謂曲則全者	When the ancients said, "Warped therefore intact,"

豈虛言哉　　　　　　　It was no empty talk.

誠全而歸之　　　　　　For truly the whole returns intact.

COMMENTARY ....

This chapter begins with a highly succinct stanza made up of six three-character lines. The pivot of each line is the form word 則 (*zé*), suggesting causality similar to the English "therefore." From a commonsensical point of view, such a proposition as "something is bent and therefore keeps straight" seems self-contradictory. It would make much better sense to replace "and therefore" with "but." Upon closer examination, however, you find profound truth in these seemingly absurd statements. If a piece of material allows itself to be bent and twisted, it stays whole. If it resists bending, it snaps. By the same token, if something gets warped, it still has a good chance of remaining intact. If it resists, it cracks. That's why the Lord of the River's commentaries to the first line read, "Bend yourself backwards and follow the crowd, do not be obstinate, and you will keep yourself intact." So what seems absurd turns out to be quite commonsensical. My translation tries to mimic the highly condensed syntax as well as the logical tension of the original.

23

希言自然。

故飘风不终朝，骤雨不终日。孰为此者？天地。天地尚不能久，而况于人乎？

故从事于道者，同于道；德者，同于德；失者，同于失。同于道者，道亦乐得之；同于德者，德亦乐得之；同于失者，失亦乐得之。

希言自然	Use few words and let things be.
故飄風不終朝	Thus, strong winds do not last the entire morning;
驟雨不終日	Torrential rains do not last the whole day.
孰爲此者	Who made this so?
天地	Heaven and Earth.
天地尚不能久	If Heaven and Earth cannot make these last,
而況於人乎	How can Man?
故從事於道者同於道	Therefore those who practice *Dao* identify with *Dao*;
德者同於德	Those who practice *De* identify with *De*;
失者同於失	Those who lack both identify with the lack.
同於道者	If you identify with *Dao*,
道亦樂得之	*Dao* is glad to have you.
同於德者	If you identify with *De*,
德亦樂得之	*De* is glad to have you.
同於失者	If you identify with the lack,
失亦樂得之	The lack is also glad to have you.

COMMENTARY ....

The first line stands apart as a stanza by itself. Some redactors think it does not belong here and therefore leave it out. But it actually epitomizes one of Laozi's favorite motifs and forms a striking headnote for the case he tries to make. Again, drawing his analogies from Nature, Laozi cites the fact that one does not need to waste words complaining about a sudden gale or a pouring rainstorm because they never last long. He invokes the patient attitude of Heaven and Earth to let such natural events come and go as a model for human behavior. In one's quest for *Dao* and *De*, all one has to do is to identify oneself with the behavior of *Dao* and *De* via that of Heaven and Earth. If one gets it, one gets it. If one doesn't, one doesn't. No words are necessary.

In the second half of this chapter, the character 樂 (*lè*) (glad) appears three times, catching the eye of the readers for its vivid personification of the otherwise abstract concepts of *Dao* and *De* and the lack thereof. I did not see this character in either the received version or the Mawangdui scripts but found it in *Laozi's Dao De Jing with He Shang Gong's Line-by-Line Commentaries*. I gladly accepted this as a welcome addition. The interesting thing is that, according to this version, not only are *Dao* and *De* glad to have those who come to their embrace, but the absence of *Dao* and *De* is also glad to see those who stay away from the pair. It is all up to us to decide which way to go. *Dao* and *De* never impose. In a sense this is also a fair warning to those who are hesitating to embrace these supreme powers.

24

....

企者不立；跨者不行。自见者不明；自是者不彰；自伐者无功；自矜者不长。

其在道也，曰余食赘形、物或恶之，故有道者不处。

企者不立	You cannot keep standing on tiptoe;
跨者不行	You cannot keep walking in strides.
自見者不明	He who exhibits himself is not apparent;
自是者不彰	He who justifies himself is not evident;
自伐者無功	He who brags deserves no credit;
自矜者不長	He who is arrogant cannot last.
其在道也	From the point of view of *Dao*
曰餘食贅形	These are called surplus food and unwanted fat,
物或惡之	Which people abhor
故有道者不處	And those attaining *Dao* avoid.

COMMENTARY ....

Laozi adopts a three-tiered rhetoric to make his point. He begins by drawing attention to some obvious, natural, or everyday phenomenon, such as the futility of attempting to keep on standing on tiptoe or walking in strides. He then goes on to reveal the irony behind some less obvious but still easily discernable patterns in human behavior, such as the self-defeating attempts at self-aggrandizement. Last, he takes us to a still deeper level of understanding the human condition, namely, seeing things from the point of view of *Dao*. From that perspective, all those attempts are abominable and should be avoided. This chapter may be considered a sequel to the previous one in that it points out the irreconcilability between the humility of *Dao* and the superfluous use of words to promote oneself. It is also an echo of the second stanza of chapter 22.

25

....

有物混成，先天地生。寂兮寥兮、独立不改，周行而不殆，可以为天下母。吾不知其名，字之曰道，强为之名曰大。大曰逝；逝曰远；远曰反。

故道大、天大、地大、人亦大。域中有四大，而人居其一焉。

人法地；地法天；天法道；道法自然。

有物混成   There was something undifferentiated and yet complete,

先天地生   Born before Heaven and Earth,

寂兮寥兮   Soundless and formless,

獨立不改   Independent and unchanging.

周行而不殆   Revolving endlessly,

可以爲天下母   It may be thought of as the Mother of all under Heaven.

吾不知其名   I do not know its name;

字之曰道   So I just call it *Dao*,

强爲之名曰大   And arbitrarily name it Great.

大曰逝   To be Great means to move on and on;

逝曰遠   To move on and on means to go far and wide;

遠曰反   To go far and wide means to return.

故   Thus,

道大   *Dao* is great;

天大   Heaven is great;

地大   Earth is great;

人亦大   Man is also great.

域中有四大　　　　The universe has four great ones,
而人居其一焉　　　And Man is one of them.

人法地　　　　　　Man follows the ways of Earth;
地法天　　　　　　Earth follows the ways of Heaven;
天法道　　　　　　Heaven follows the ways of *Dao*;
道法自然　　　　　*Dao* follows its own ways.

COMMENTARY ....

This chapter is arguably the core of the entire *Daodejing* in that it embodies Laozi's boldest elucidation of the *Dao*-centered cosmos. Its language, however, is so simple that it hardly needs explication. Nonetheless, it incorporates all the defining features of *Dao* that deserve our close study and contemplation.

- First of all, it is a thing, a substantive something, not an abstract idea.
- It precedes Heaven and Earth and is the absolute supreme being.
- It is invisible, inaudible, and intangible but does exist.
- It keeps moving and is the prime mover of the universe.
- Its motion is characterized by its ceaseless cycle of go and return.
- It is female and the mother of all things.
- It has no name except the arbitrary appellation of *Dao* imposed by humans.
- It is totally independent of human will or the will of other beings.
- It follows its own ways and laws, which in turn govern the behavior of the cosmos.

The last line, 道法自然 (*dào fǎ zì rán*) (Dao follows its own ways), may be considered the core of cores. As I explained in my commentary on chapter 17, 自 (*zi*) means "self" and 然 (*rán*) means "so" or "as such." To translate this line as "*Dao* follows Nature" would place *Dao* under Nature as the second in command and thereby create a fifth domain, which would be totally out of place in the Daoist cosmology.

26

重为轻根，静为躁君。是以君子终日行不离辎重。虽有荣观，燕处超然。奈何万乘之主，而以身轻天下？

轻则失根，躁则失君。

重爲輕根	What is heavy weights down what is light;
静爲躁君	What is still reins in what is restless.
是以	That is why
君子終日行不離輜重	A wise traveler never walks away from his luggage van.
雖有榮觀	Though he possesses luxurious mansions,
燕處超然	He lives in peace and stays aloof.
奈何萬乘之主	Why would an owner of ten thousand chariots
而以身輕天下	Treat his own life lightly when governing the world?
輕則失根	Be light-headed and you lose your root;
躁則失君	Get restless and you lose your control.

COMMENTARY

Laozi uses the word 根 (gēn) or "root" to refer to its function as anchor. Just as a kite needs to be held down by a firm hand, people need a sturdy mind to weight down their light-headedness. By the same token they need a quiet mentor to keep them from getting restless. That is the way Laozi thinks a man of wealth and power should conduct his life. He should stay close to his properties and live a peaceful life. However, Laozi laments the reality of feudal rulers wasting their life on rash and frivolous acts. In the age of the Warring States, the ruler of a big feudal state could own as many as ten thousand chariots and carriages, the ruler of a lesser state could own a thousand chariots, and so forth. Laozi could not understand why even the most powerful ruler would still live in such a thoughtless manner. He ends the chapter by warning against the danger of losing one's anchor and self-control.

27

善行无辙迹；善言无瑕谪；善数不用筹策；善闭无关楗而不可开；善结无绳约而不可解。

是以圣人常善救人，故无弃人；常善救物，故无弃物。是谓袭明。

故善人者，不善人之师；不善人者，善人之资。不贵其师，不爱其资，虽智大迷，是谓要妙。

善行無轍迹	A good driver never leaves behind a trace of his rut;
善言無瑕	A good speaker never commits a slip of the tongue;
善數不用籌策	A good accountant needs no tallies or counters.
善閉無關楗而不可開	A good fastener uses no latch or bolt but cannot be opened;
善結無繩約而不可解	A good knot uses no rope or noose but cannot be untied.

是以	That is how
聖人常善救人	The sage is always good at saving people
故無棄人	So that no one is abandoned;
常善救物	He is always good at saving things
故無棄物	So that nothing is abandoned.
是謂襲明	That is called the heritage of wisdom.

故善人者	Thus those who are good
不善人之師	Are teachers to those who are not so good;
不善人者	Those who are not so good
善人之資	Are object lessons for those who are good.
不貴其師	If you do not value your teachers,
不愛其資	If you do not cherish your object lessons,

雖智大迷　　　　No matter how knowledgeable, you are totally lost.
是謂要妙　　　　That is the profound truth.

COMMENTARY ....

Like chapter 8, this chapter is about "good." But the focus here seems to be on "being good at" rather than "being good." The first stanza illustrates the point that being good at something is not so much a matter of skill or technology as getting the wisdom behind it. The second stanza takes this a step further to the level of the sage. A sage is not just a person with a good heart out to save people. He has to be good at saving people so that his good wishes can be fulfilled. That is what Laozi calls the heritage of wisdom. It is another example where Laozi's emphasis is not on morality but on efficacy, on Daoist wisdom as opposed to Confucian compassion.

The last stanza takes the readers in a new direction. After examining the meanings of "good," he wants us to think about the "not good" since everything has its opposite, as chapter 2 amply illustrates. Laozi thinks that both the good and the not good can be put to good use by cherishing one as teachers and the other as object lessons. In the end, there is really no one or nothing that is abandoned for being no good. If we can achieve that, we have reached the heart of "profound truth." Note that Laozi does not say "good and bad" but only "good and not good." If we stretch this a little in our translation, we should probably say "good and not so good."

28

知其雄，守其雌，为天下溪。为天下溪，常德不离，复归于婴儿。

知其白，守其辱，为天下谷。为天下谷，常德乃足，复归于朴。

朴散则为器，圣人用之，则为官长。故大制不割。

知其雄	Know the male,
守其雌	Stay with the female,
爲天下谿	Be the ravine of the world.
爲天下谿	Be the ravine of the world,
常德不離	And the Eternal *De* will never leave you;
復歸於嬰兒	And you will return to infancy.
知其白	Know the light,
守其辱	Stay with the dark,
爲天下谷	Be the valley of the world.
爲天下谷	Be the valley of the world,
常德乃足	And the Eternal *De* will always satisfy you;
復歸於樸	And you will return to the pristine timber.
樸散則爲器	Raw timber scattered becomes utensils.
聖人用之	The sage uses them
則爲官長	And becomes the leader of leaders.
故大制不割	Thus, a great regime is undivided.

COMMENTARY ....

Laozi speaks of "the Eternal *De*" or 常德 (*cháng dé*) the way he speaks of the "Eternal *Dao*" as opposed to the various ordinary ways that pass off as *dao*. In the same vein Laozi qualifies the *De* he speaks of with the adjective "eternal" or "great" to distinguish it from the lesser virtues. As the emanation of *Dao*, the Eternal *De* embodies the sum total of all the defining features of *Dao*: the feminine as opposed to the masculine; the dark as opposed to the light; the valley and ravine, which symbolize humility and receptivity; and the infant and the pristine timber symbolizing the innocent beginnings of life. Laozi urges people to stand by these features but does not rule out the collateral existence of their opposites. Thus he wants people to know the masculine and the light while staying with the feminine and the dark or profound.

Another concept that is underscored here is "return" as in "return to infancy" and "return to the pristine timber." Laozi highlights this in chapter 25 as part of the incessant motion of *Dao*. Interestingly enough, once things return to their roots, they are on the go again, and they spread far and wide till they again return to the roots. Since the return is not the final destination, Laozi gives us in the second stanza a glimpse of the new cycle. He points out that as the pristine timber spreads out, it takes the form of utensils so the sage ruler can put them to use. That is how he commands his state as the leader of leaders. His is a great regime that is undivided because it stays with the pristine one.

. . . .

29

将欲取天下而为之，吾见其不得已。天下神器，不可为也，不可执也。为者败之，执者失之。

是以圣人无为故无败；无执，故无失。

夫物或行或随；或歔或吹；或强或羸；或培或隳。

是以圣人去甚，去奢，去泰。

將欲取天下而爲之	Wanting to win the world and acting upon it—
吾見其不得已	To me this is not going to work.
天下神器	The world is a sacred vessel,
不可爲也	It cannot be acted upon,
不可執也	It cannot be held on to.
爲者敗之	Those who act upon it will fail,
執者失之	Those who hold on to it will lose.
是以聖人無爲	That is why the sage practices Non-doing
故無敗	And therefore does not fail;
無執	He does not hold,
故無失	And therefore does not lose.
夫物或行或隨	For some prefer to go on their own, others prefer to follow;
或歔或吹	Some breathe gently, some blow hard;
或強或羸	Some are strong, some fragile;
或培或隳	Some self-increment, some self-destruct.

是以聖人去甚	That is why the sage refuses to be excessive,
去奢	Or extravagant,
去泰	Or extreme.

COMMENTARY ....

Here Laozi continues to advocate the principle of *wuwei* or Non-doing and its application to politics. He brings two new things to the subject. One is the idea that the world is a sacred vessel. It is a powerful testimony to the deep humility that Laozi thinks a sage ruler should feel toward the world. Woe to the one who attempts to manipulate or hold on to the world he is supposed to lead. The other thing is Laozi's recognition of the diversity of human inclinations. The examples are taken from everyday human behavior; the lesson they teach is that the ruler should let things be and refrain from leaning toward one extreme or the other.

30

以道佐人主者，不以兵强天下。其事好还。师之所处，荆棘生焉。大军之后，必有凶年。

善有果而已，不以取强。果而勿矜，果而勿伐，果而勿骄，果而不得已，果而勿强。

物壮则老，是谓不道，不道早已。

以道佐人主者	He who assists a ruler with *Dao*,
不以兵强天下	Does not use weapons to coerce the world.
其事好還	For that is sure to rebound.
師之所處	Where troops were stationed,
荆棘生焉	Brambles will grow;
大軍之後	After a major war
必有凶年	There will be famine.
善有果而已	It's all a matter of being good at gaining results,
不以取強	Not winning by force.
果而勿矜	Results gained, yet not arrogant,
果而勿伐	Results gained, yet not boastful,
果而勿驕	Results gained, yet not proud,
果而不得已	Results gained, yet with reluctance,
果而勿強	Results gained, yet not by force.
物壯則老	Things that resort to force age fast.
是謂不道	That is called going against *Dao*.
不道早已	Going against *Dao* brings early demise.

COMMENTARY ···

This is the first time Laozi invokes the term 兵 (*bīng*) or arms/weapons. It is a topic of deep concern for him as he lived at a time when the Chinese nation had been ridden with feudal wars for hundreds of years with no sign of an ending in sight.

Obviously Laozi is opposed to the use of force, but he does not condemn it from an ethical point of view. Rather he adopts a pragmatic approach, focusing on the result or 果 (*guǒ*), a word he repeats over and over in the second stanza. In other words, he tries to persuade the feudal rulers to change their attitude and the means they adopt without denying their worldly ambitions totally. You might think Laozi is trying to appeal to the rulers' self-interest, but his recommendation is based on his understanding of the nonviolent, non-ethical power of *Dao*. If one acknowledges this power and follows its ways, one naturally wins. If one goes against it, one suffers early demise.

31

夫兵者，不祥之器，物或恶之，故有道者不处。

君子居则贵左；用兵则贵右。兵者不祥之器，非君子之器，不得已而用之，恬淡为上。

胜而不美，而美之者，是乐杀人。夫乐杀人者，则不可得志于天下矣。吉事尚左，凶事尚右。偏将军居左，上将军居右。言以丧礼处之。杀人之众，以悲哀泣之。战胜以丧礼处之。

夫兵者不祥之器	The fact is that weapons are ominous vessels,
物或恶之	Which people abhor,
故有道者不處	And those attaining *Dao* avoid.
君子居則貴左	In times of peace, men of honor esteem the left;
用兵則貴右	When it comes to using arms they esteem the right.
兵者不祥之器	For arms are ominous utensils
非君子之器	Not the vessels of men of honor.
不得已而用之	They are used only as the last resort,
恬淡爲上	And should preferably be treated lightly.
勝而不美	A victory is not to be glorified;
而美之者	Those who glorify a victory
是樂殺人	Are gloating over killing human beings.
夫樂殺人者	And those who gloat over killing people
則不可得志於天下矣	Must not be granted their worldly ambitions.
吉事尚左	On happy occasions the left is the upper hand;
凶事尚右	On woeful occasions the right is the upper hand.
偏將軍居左	The lieutenant general is positioned on the left;

上將軍居右	The general is positioned on the right.
言以喪禮處之	That is how a funeral ceremony is conducted.
殺人之眾	With multitudes slaughtered,
以悲哀泣之	One should grieve over the occasion.
戰勝以喪禮處之	The victory should be treated as a funeral.

COMMENTARY

If the last chapter is a gentle admonition to would-be conquerors to refrain from use of force, this one is a stern rebuke of those who celebrate the victories of violence. Apparently in Laozi's time, such celebrations must have been quite frequent and the old man must have been deeply disturbed by this phenomenon. When he accuses these victors of "gloating over killing people," you can almost feel the heat of his outrage. However, given the circumstances, he still does not rule out the possibility of some use of force. But he urges that it be treated as a last resort and handled in a low-key manner. Instead of celebration, he suggests victories should be treated like funerals. Again, when we hear Laozi say, "With multitudes slaughtered, one should grieve over the occasion," we can feel the emotional pitch of the old man's grief for the loss of lives. If any of us still has a lingering doubt as to why Laozi says in chapter 5, "The sage is not humane, he treats all people like straw dogs," we can see here that the wise old man is certainly not unfeeling. This aspect of Laozi's personality will emerge again and again in later chapters.

32

道常无名朴。虽小，天下莫能臣。侯王若能守之，万物将自宾。

天地相合，以降甘露，民莫之令而自均。

始制有名。名亦既有，夫亦将知止。知止可以不殆。

譬道之在天下，犹川谷之于江海。

道常無名樸　　　　*Dao* in its eternity is the nameless pristine timber.
雖小　　　　　　　Though small,
天下莫能臣　　　　No one in this world can subdue it.
侯王若能守之　　　If lords and kings can abide by it,
萬物將自賓　　　　All things will submit themselves.

天地相合　　　　　When Heaven and Earth copulate,
以降甘露　　　　　Sweet dewdrops fall.
民莫之令而自均　　People share them equally without being told to.

始制有名　　　　　When things begin to grow, they take on names.
名亦既有　　　　　As names are established,
夫亦將知止　　　　They know their limits.
知止可以不殆　　　Knowing their limits, they avoid hazards.

譬道之在天下　　　For the world is to *Dao*,
猶川谷之於江海　　What brooks and ravines are to the rivers and seas.

· 72 ·

COMMENTARY ....

Having expressed his strong disapproval of the use of force in the previous chapters, Laozi goes back to the power of *Dao*. He assures the feudal lords that as long as they adhere to *Dao*, all things under Heaven will submit themselves.

In the first three stanzas *Dao* presents itself in three phases:

- First, in its pristine state. Laozi uses the metaphor of 樸 (*pǔ*), a piece of simple raw timber, uncut and unadorned. It has no name and is humble and small, so much that it is invisible. Yet it is charged with latent power.
- Second, as Heaven and Earth. Through their copulation, *Dao* spreads itself as dewdrops to nurture all things in the world.
- Third, as things. When *Dao* manifests itself as "all things under Heaven," it creates an order with names attached to them. With these names, everything knows its place and there are no troubles.

The chapter ends with Laozi's favorite analogy of water that gathers its momentum and power as it flows from the tributaries into the rivers and seas.

33

知人者智，自知者明。胜人者有力，自胜者强。

知足者富。强行者有志。不失其所者久。死而不亡者寿。

知人者智	He who knows others is intelligent;
自知者明	He who knows himself is enlightened.
勝人者有力	He who overcomes others shows might;
自勝者強	He who overcomes himself shows strength.
知足者富	He who is content is rich.
強行者有志	He who is diligent has will.
不失其所者久	He who does not lose his foundation endures.
死而不亡者壽	He who dies but never vanishes enjoys longevity.

COMMENTARY

From governing the world to self-governance, Laozi brings *Dao* to the ground level of self-cultivation. Here the commentaries of the Lord of the River may prove especially useful. He points out that by "knowing oneself" Laozi means knowing one's gifts as well as one's defects. A person with such self-knowledge hears no noise and sees no form in his inner self. Such a person is thoroughly enlightened (明 *mìng*). The Lord of the River also points out that to overcome oneself means to overcome one's emotions and desires. "If a person can accomplish that, no one in this world can compete with him."

Following this line of thinking, "to not lose one's foundation" means "to conserve and nourish oneself so that one does not lose the essential vital energy he has received from Heaven."

The last line is interpreted differently depending largely on different readings of the character 亡 (*wáng*). Wang Bi (226–249), known for his authoritative redactions and annotations of *Laozi* and *Yi Jing*, takes the character 亡 (*wáng*) literally to mean "vanish" or "disappear." His interpretation of the last line is, "One who dies but is not destroyed has longevity." Wang says in his notes, "Although one dies, thanks to the *Dao* by which he lives, he is not destroyed, and that is how he manages to enjoy longevity to the full." (Lynn 1999, 111) The Mawangdui versions, however, read the character 亡 (*wáng*) as a variant of 忘 (*wàng*), meaning "to forget." Thus, the line would mean, "He who dies but is not forgotten enjoys longevity." The Lord of the River, on the other hand, thinks 亡 is homonymous with 妄 (*wàng*), meaning "wanton" or "unrestrained." His reading of the line is, "If one does not gaze, listen and chatter without restraint, he has no grudge against the world till his death and will therefore live a long life."

大道泛兮，其可左右。万物恃之以生而不辞，功成而不有。衣养万物而不为主，可名于小。万物归焉而不为主；可名为大。以其终不自为大，故能成其大。

大道氾兮	The great *Dao* overflows;
其可左右	It can go left, it can go right.
萬物恃之以生而不辭	All things depend on it for life and it never declines;
功成而不有	It accomplishes but never possesses.
衣養萬物而不爲主	It nurtures all things but never dominates;
可名於小	That may be called small.
萬物歸焉而不爲主	All things submit themselves to it but it never dominates;
可名爲大	That may be called great.
以其終不自爲大	Because it never claims its own greatness,
故能成其大	It therefore achieves greatness.

COMMENTARY

In this eulogy of *Dao*, Laozi further explains the meaning of "small" and "great." He begins by praising *Dao*'s greatness but calls it small in the sense that it is humble and never stops serving all things with humility. Then he goes back to *Dao*'s greatness not only in the sense that it wins the love and support of all things but because it never dominates and never claims greatness.

执大象，天下往。往而不害，安平太。

乐与饵，过客止。道之出口，淡乎其无味。视之不足见，听之不足闻，用之不足既。

執大象	When the Great Image is upheld,
天下往	All under Heaven flock to it.
往而不害	Flocking together but causing no harm,
安平太	All live in peace and tranquility.
樂與餌	Music and food
過客止	May make passers-by pause;
道之出口	But *Dao*, when expressed,
淡乎其無味	Tastes as bland as it is flavorless.
視之不足見	You look at it but cannot see,
聽之不足聞	You listen to it but cannot hear,
用之不足既	You use it and it cannot be exhausted.

COMMENTARY

The Great Image is *Dao*. See chapter 21, which says, "Intangible and elusive, yet it contains the Image." "Upholding the Great Image" means adhering to *Dao*. When multitudes of people flock together as a mob, it usually signals unrest. But when people rally around the great *Dao*, it means peace and tranquility.

The second stanza seems to anticipate the question, "Why is that?" In other words, what makes *Dao* so attractive and powerful? Again Laozi falls back on the intangibility and elusiveness of *Dao* by speaking to its tastelessness, its invisibility and inaudibility. But he does not totally elude the question because he makes it clear in the final line that despite the above, its usefulness is inexhaustible.

36

将欲歙之，必固张之；将欲弱之，必固强之；将欲废之，必固兴之；将欲取之，必固与之。是谓微明。

柔弱胜刚强。鱼不可脱于渊，国之利器不可以示人。

將欲歙之	If you want to close something,
必固張之	You must first open it.
將欲弱之	If you want to weaken something,
必固強之	You must first strengthen it.
將欲廢之	If you want to abolish something,
必固興之	You must first promote it.
將欲取之	If you want to take something,
必固與之	You must first give it.
是謂微明	That is called subtle premonition.
柔弱勝剛強	The soft and weak overcomes the hard and strong;
魚不可脫於淵	Fish cannot live out of deep water;
國之利器不可以示人	The state must not flex its muscles.

COMMENTARY

Laozi is driving home the homespun truth that when a thing reaches its extreme, it turns to its opposite. He uses the phrase 必固 (*bì gù*) or "must necessarily" repeatedly to emphasize the inevitability of this law of opposites. Understanding this inevitability is what he calls "subtle premonition." It would be unjust to Laozi to charge him with instigating conspiracy, for what he is illustrating is just what things are like in daily life as well as in state affairs. But the lesson he draws is especially applicable in a situation where a weak and defenseless state is confronted with a powerful and aggressive adversary. It is the same idea of *wuwei* (non-doing) or *buzheng* (non-contention), of yielding in order to gain and stepping back to end up in front. Applying the idea to state governance, the ruler must keep a low profile instead of showing off his power to intimidate his subjects. Refraining from showing off one's power is like letting the fish stay in deep water.

37

道常无为而无不为。侯王若能守之，万物将自化。化而欲作，吾将镇之以无名之朴。镇之以无名之朴，夫将不欲。不欲以静，天下将自正。

道常無爲	*Dao* in its eternity does nothing,
而無不爲	Yet nothing is not done.
侯王若能守之	If lords and kings can all abide by that,
萬物將自化	All things will change of themselves.
化而欲作	As they change, their desires start to grow;
吾將鎮之以無名之樸	I calm them down with the nameless pristine timber.
鎮之以無名之樸	Calmed by the nameless pristine timber,
夫將不欲	They will have no more desire.
不欲以靜	Desireless and calm,
天下將自正	The world will correct its own course.

COMMENTARY

This is an echo of chapter 32, where the nameless pristine timber is mentioned and the lords and kings are urged to abide by it. But here the emphasis shifts to the principle of "Non-doing." "Do nothing and nothing is not done." That has become one of the enduring proverbs in the Chinese language. In the context of rulership, it means that as long as the rulers refrain from any coercive action and set a model of quiet humility, "All things will change of themselves" and "The world will correct its own course." But here is the interesting point. As Laozi points out in chapter 25, *Dao* moves in a cycle. It travels far to the extreme, returns to the starting point and goes out on the swing again. He is keenly aware that after changing for the better, people's desires may start growing again. So they need to be calmed again by the simple truth of the pristine timber. Once their desires are under control, the world will take care of itself and things will go right again.

Part Two:
De

··

38

上德不德，是以有德；下德不失德；是以无德。

上德无为而无以为；上仁为之而无以为；上义为之而有以为。上礼为之而莫之应，则攘臂而扔之。

故失道而后德，失德而后仁，失仁而后义，失义而后礼。

夫礼者，忠信之薄而乱之首。前识者，道之华而愚之始。

是以大丈夫处其厚不居其薄；处其实，不居其华。故去彼取其此。

上德不德	Superior *De* is not about virtue;
是以有德	It therefore has virtue;
下德不失德	Inferior *De* does not want to lose virtue;
是以無德	It therefore has no virtue.
上德無爲而無以爲	Superior *De* does nothing and has no intent of doing anything;
上仁爲之而無以爲	Superior Humaneness does something but has no intent of doing anything.
上義爲之而有以爲	Superior Righteousness does something and has the intent of doing something.
上禮爲之而莫之應	Superior Propriety does something but receives no response,
則攘臂而扔之	So it raises its arm and flexes its muscles.
故失道而後德	Thus when *Dao* is lost, there is *De*;
失德而後仁	When *De* is lost, there is Humaneness;
失仁而後義	When Humaneness is lost, there is Righteousness;
失義而後禮	When Righteousness is lost, there is Propriety.

夫禮者　　　　　　　　As for Propriety,
忠信之薄而亂之首　　　It is the paucity of faith and the beginning of turmoil;
前識者　　　　　　　　As for prophecies,
道之華而愚之始　　　　They are the embellishments of *Dao* and the
　　　　　　　　　　　beginning of folly.

是以大丈夫　　　　　　That is why a true man
處其厚不居其薄　　　　Stays with abundance and not with paucity,
處其實不居其華　　　　Stays with substance and not with embellishments.
故去彼取其此　　　　　Hence, he discards that and adopts this.

COMMENTARY ....

Laozi begins this chapter on *De* by posing a serious challenge to the popular concept of *De* as moral virtue. He proclaims his own concept of *De* as superior precisely because his *De* is not about virtue. In contrast, he debunks the much touted moral excellence as an inferior variety of *De* at best. The yardstick he uses to distinguish these two kinds of *De*, or virtue, if you will, is the benchmark principle of *wuwei* or Non-doing. Put plainly, if you are afraid of losing your virtue and wear it on your sleeve all the time, that goes against the principle of *wuwei* and therefore has no virtue. But if you live your life according to *Dao* and are not mindful of having or losing virtue, you are like *Dao* that "does nothing and has no intent of doing anything." That means you have attained virtue of the superior kind.

Having made this crucial distinction, Laozi moves on to examine the three most valued virtues in the common moral code, namely, 仁 (*rén*), meaning "humaneness" or "benevolence"; 義 (*yì*), meaning "duty" or "righteousness"; and 禮 (lǐ), meaning "ritual" or "propriety." But he is not going to discuss them in terms of ethics. What he does is judge them unequivocally by the standard of *wuwei*.

The character 仁 (rén), as I explained in chapter 5, consists of two parts. The part on the left is the "human" radical; the part on the right is the character 二 (èr) for "two." This suggests that the character has to do with human relations. It is safe to say that the question most frequently asked of Confucius throughout the *Analects* is about 仁. One of the answers Confucius gives is simply: "Love people." Another answer says, "What you do not wish for yourself, do not impose upon others." And so forth. Presumably the one who practices *ren* does so with no intent of accomplishing anything. It is a good virtue but does not fully meet the criteria of *wuwei*.

The character 義 or "righteousness" has 羊 (yáng) or "sheep" at the top and 我 (wǒ) or "I/me" at the bottom. It gives the idea of a shepherd who carries his sheep on his shoulders and cares for it both as his responsibility and his possession. Whoever exercises this virtue always feels duty-bound and wants to be seen as a protector of social justice. But by such a conscious demonstration of self-will, this virtue fails the test of *wuwei*.

Last but not least is 禮 or "propriety." It means conducting oneself according to the code of rituals. In another answer about 仁, Confucius delivers his famous saying, "Restrain the self and restore the rites; that is what humaneness is about." Confucius grew up near a graveyard and loved watching rituals of ancestral worship being performed there. But rites are not just a set of ceremonies or a book of etiquette to be observed by polite society. Confucius sets great store by rituals and rites because these are operable, measurable, verifiable yardsticks for moral awareness or sense of propriety. If the time-honored rites cease to be observed, that is symptomatic of the moral degradation of society. In a broader sense, this measurable moral code also includes the penalties for violations. So, as Laozi bluntly points out, *li* or propriety takes not only deliberate but coercive action to enforce ethical values, and the result runs counter to what such actions anticipate. That is what Laozi means when he ridicules *li* for taking action and, when receiving no response, raising its arms and flexing its muscles. That is also why he says that *li* "marks the paucity of faith and the beginning of turmoil."

Taken at their face value, all the above judgments may sound highly subjective. But the point is that Laozi simply refuses to be drawn into the discourse and terminology of Confucian ethics. In fact, nowhere in the entire *Daodejing* does Laozi promote such ethical values as humaneness and righteousness. Whenever he invokes those terms, he is just using them as foil to his own concepts of *Dao* and *De*.

Laozi uses the character 華 (*huá*) or "flowers" for "embellishments" and 實 (*shí*) or "fruit" for "substance." He encourages "true men" (a rare slip of male chauvinism for Laozi) to discard the embellishments and embrace the substance.

Incidentally Laozi throws in a comment on those prophets who claim clairvoyance in the name of *Dao*. He warns people that those are just embellishments of *Dao*, and should you believe in them you would embark on the path of folly.

39

昔之得一者：天得一以清；地得一以宁；神得一以灵；谷得一以盈；万物得一以生；侯王得一以为天下正。

其致之也，谓天无以清，将恐裂；地无以宁，将恐废；神无以灵，将恐歇；谷无以盈，将恐竭；万物无以生，将恐灭；侯王无以正，将恐蹶。

故贵以贱为本，高以下为基。是以侯王自称孤、寡、不榖。此非以贱为本邪？非乎？故至誉无誉。是故不欲琭琭如玉，珞珞如石。

昔之得一者	Look at those in the past who attained the One:
天得一以清	Heaven, having attained the One, was clear;
地得一以寧	Earth, having attained the One, was tranquil;
神得一以靈	The Spirit, having attained the One, was potent;
谷得一以盈	The valleys, having attained the One, were plentiful;
萬物得一以生	All things, having attained the One, were able to live;
侯王得一以爲天下正	Lords and kings, having attained the One, set the norm for the world.
其致之也	If we push this further,
謂天無以清	We may say that if Heaven was not clear,
將恐裂	It would probably collapse;
地無以寧	If Earth was not tranquil,
將恐廢	It would probably be destroyed;
神無以靈	If the Spirit was not potent,
將恐歇	It would probably cease to work;
谷無以盈	If the valleys were not plentiful,
將恐竭	They would probably dry up;
萬物無以生	If all things had nothing to live by,
將恐滅	They would probably become extinct;

| 侯王無以正 | If the lords and kings had lost their norm, |
| 將恐蹶 | They would probably fall. |

故貴以賤爲本	Thus the noble depends on the humble as the roots;
高以下爲基	The high depends on the low as the base;
是以侯王自稱孤寡不穀	That is why the lords and kings call themselves the Orphaned, the Widowed, or the Undeserving.
此非以賤爲本邪	Isn't that taking the lowly as the roots?
非乎	Isn't that so?
故至譽無譽	Thus the highest honor is no honor.
是故不欲琭琭如玉	Therefore do not desire jade-like glamour,
珞珞如石	But rock-like solidity.

COMMENTARY

This chapter opens a whole new dimension to the meaning of *De*, free from all the trappings of the ethical discourse. The character 德 (*dé*) is homonymous and sometimes interchangeable with the character 得 (*dé*), meaning "get," "receive," "reach," or "attain." So when Laozi talks about Superior *De*, he is not thinking about the high-sounding virtues but simply the prospect of attaining *Dao* or "getting it." Attaining the One means attaining *Dao*, just like "embracing the One" and "adhering to the One." Laozi harkens back to an idealized past when *Dao* was embraced by everything in the universe, from Heaven to Earth to all beings, resulting in peace and prosperity for all. In case his audience fails to be inspired, he makes an urgent appeal by alerting people to the dire consequences of not abiding by *Dao*. Such a warning was fully justified historically, given the turmoil and devastation the world was already experiencing.

In the last two stanzas Laozi reminds his readers that to reach for *Dao* means to go back to one's humble roots, to be in the company of the lowly, to look for substance, not glamour.

40

反者道之动；弱者道之用。天下万物生于有，有生于无。

反者道之動	Return is *Dao*'s motion;
弱者道之用	Weakness is *Dao*'s application.
天下萬物生於有	All things under Heaven are born of Being;
有生於無	Being is born of Nonbeing.

COMMENTARY

This is the shortest chapter in the entire *Daodejing* but takes the lengthy discussions about *De* back to the fundamentals of *Dao*. The first character 反 (*fǎn*) actually has two related meanings. One is "return," also written as 返 (*fǎn*), and the other is "opposite." When a thing reaches its extreme, it necessarily goes back to its opposite. This is *Dao*'s infallible law of motion. Weakness, synonymous with softness and humility, is exactly where the power of *Dao* lies in its application. Laozi concludes this short chapter with the sobering reminder, "Being is born of Nonbeing." That, to him, is the ultimate truth.

41

上士闻道，勤而行之；中士闻道，若存若亡；下士闻道，大笑之。不笑不足以为道。

故建言有之：明道若昧；进道若退；夷道若颣。

上德若谷；广德若不足；建德若偷；质真若渝。

大白若辱；大方无隅；大器晚成；大音希声；大象无形。

道隐无名；夫唯道善贷且成。

上士聞道	When the best student hears about *Dao*,
勤而行之	He applies it diligently.
中士聞道	When the average student hears about *Dao*,
若存若亡	He seems to get it one moment and miss it the next.
下士聞道	When the slow student hears about *Dao*,
大笑之	He laughs at it.
不笑不足以爲道	Without that laugh, it would not be *Dao*.
故建言有之	Thus here are some sayings:
明道若昧	Understanding *Dao* is like befuddlement;
進道若退	Progress in *Dao* is like moving backwards;
夷道若纇	The smooth road to *Dao* is like a rugged path.
上德若谷	Superior *De* seems like a valley;
廣德若不足	Abundant *De* seems unfulfilled;
建德若偷	Robust *De* seems indolent;
質真若渝	The pristine and pure seems volatile.

大白若辱	Great clarity is like turbidity;
大方無隅	Great squares have no corners;
大器晚成	Great vessels are completed late;
大音希聲	Great music has little sound;
大象無形	Great Image has no form.
道隱無名	*Dao* is hidden and has no name;
夫唯道善貸且成	For only *Dao* is good at giving and achieving.

COMMENTARY ....

If attaining *Dao* means attaining the state of *wuwei* or Non-doing, why does it require diligent practice? The fact of the matter is that the truth of *Dao* is often not apparent to everyone in its manifestations. The best student of *Dao* gets it immediately and, feeling humbled, goes right on to apply it in real life. The average student, on the other hand, is more often puzzled than enlightened, while the slow one laughs at the seeming absurdity of the stark truth. His laughter serves as a footnote to the profundity of *Dao*. *Dao* is simple and easy, but many miss the point and dismiss it by scoffing.

Traditionally, Chinese society followed the hierarchical order of 士 *shi* (scholar), 農 *nong* (farmer), 工 *gong* (worker), and 商 *shang* (merchant). Only the shi would have access to any form of education. A member of the *shi* class engaging in studies of one kind or another may be called a student. Students may be ranked as 上 (*shàng*) or superior, 中 (*zhōng*) or average, and 下 (*xià*) or inferior. That is why I translated the Chinese terms 上士 (*shàng shi*), 中士 (*zhōng shi*), and 下士 (*xià shi*) as "the best student," "the average student," and "the slow student," respectively.

The next three stanzas consist of twelve paradoxical sayings about the nature of *Dao* and *De*. Eight of these sayings contain the character 若 (*ruò*) meaning "is like" or "seems like" or "looks as if," which serves to highlight the seeming contradiction between appearance and reality. It would be a good exercise if you took some time contemplating the truthfulness of each of the "A is like B" statements. Here I will just give some clues to each of the three stanzas.

The first three sayings are all about 道 or *Dao*. Why "Understanding *Dao* is like befuddlement"? If understanding *Dao* means appreciating its infinite complexity, then you will definitely come away feeling more humbled and perplexed than when you first went in. That explains why in chapter 20 Laozi says, "The world thinks everything is crystal clear; I alone am dull and dumb." On the other hand, if you come away feeling that everything is now clear, it is a sure sign that you are still befuddled.

The next stanza is all about 德 or *De*. But according to the received version, the last line "質真若渝 (*zhì zhēn ruò yú*)" or "The pristine and pure seems volatile," does not contain the character 德 or *De*. One commentator thinks the character 真 (*zhēn*), which now fills the space where 德 should be, may be a corruption of the character 惪 (*dé*), which is an obsolete variant of 德. Indeed you do find 惪 for 德 in the Guodian bamboo script. If so, the character 德 should be restored and the line should be read, "質德若渝" or "The pristine *De* seems volatile." We remember *Dao* is in constant motion and therefore elusive and changeable. Since *De* is the emanation of *Dao* and follows the ways of *Dao*, the vintage *De* should not be static but in a constant state of change too. As for "Superior *De*" and "Abundant *De*," since they are always humble and always giving, they seem as lowly as the valleys that never feel content with their givings.

The next stanza begins each line with the character 大 (*dà*) for "big" or "great." Here Laozi is not just speaking in terms of size but a magnitude of *Dao*-like proportions. It is greatness beyond the pale of sensory perceptions or human imagination. The first line, "Great clarity is like turbidity," according to all existing versions, is placed as the second line of the previous stanza. But judging by the fact that it begins with the character 大 (*dà*) like all the lines in the penultimate stanza, it seems quite appropriate to stay where it is now.

Laozi concludes the chapter with two lines that seem to sum up the archetypical paradox of *Dao*, namely, *Dao* lies low and seems empty but is the greatest giver and achiever.

42

道生一，一生二，二生三，三生万物。万物负阴而抱阳，冲气以为和。

道生一	*Dao* gives birth to One;
一生二	One gives birth to Two;
二生三	Two gives birth to Three;
三生萬物	Three gives birth to Ten Thousand things.
萬物負陰而抱陽	All things have Yin on their back and Yang in their embrace;
沖氣以爲和	The *Qi* of the two converge and become harmony.

COMMENTARY

This chapter is best read in connection with chapter 25 to appreciate Laozi's Daoist cosmogony. In its original, formless state, *Dao* is Nonbeing. When Nonbeing takes on form but still remains undifferentiated, it becomes Being, which is the chaotic One. One bifurcates into Heaven and Earth, which in turn form the interactive domains of Yin and Yang. That is the Two. When Yin (female) and Yang (male) exchange their vital energy (*Qi*) and copulate, the Two generates the Three, a symbolic number for plurality. Multiply this process generation after generation and the Three becomes the Ten Thousand or myriad things.

All living beings, as Laozi would have observed, love to sit with their backs to the north and the front facing south. In other words, they all prefer to have Yin or the shade on their back and Yang or the sun in front. Another theory says the back, being exposed, belongs to the Yang domain while the front, being covered, belongs to the Yin domain. In any event the

Qi or vital energy of these two domains dances around in a harmonious interflow.

It is worth noting that this is the only instance where Laozi uses the terms Yin and Yang. Instead of these, he prefers the cosmological terms of Heaven and Earth and the animalistic terms of 牝 (*pin*) (female) and 牡 (*mǔ*) (male). In other chapters, he also uses the terms 雌 (*cí*) and 雄 (*xióng*), terms for female and male animals only. This choice of terminology suggests that Laozi prefers to rely more on his observations of natural phenomena than on existing abstract concepts.

43

天下之至柔，驰骋天下之至坚。无有入无间，吾是以知无为之有益。

不言之教，无为之益，天下希及之。

天下之至柔	The world's softest
馳騁天下之至堅	Prevails over the world's hardest.
無有入無間	The formless penetrates the seamless.
吾是以知無爲之有益	That is how I came to know the advantage of Non-doing.

不言之教	Teaching without words,
無爲之益	Benefiting by Non-doing—
天下希及之	Few in this world could emulate that.

COMMENTARY

As the Lord of the River points out in his commentaries on this chapter, nothing under Heaven is softer than water, and nothing under Heaven is harder than metal and rock. Water is so soft that it has no form or will to prevail. Metal or rock is so hard that it has absolutely no crack or willingness to give in. But water drips effortlessly and continuously on a piece of metal or rock until it penetrates the material. This natural phenomenon is a vivid example of the power of *wuwei* (Non-doing) as well as the power of teaching without words.

44

名与身孰亲？身与货孰多？得与亡孰病？

甚爱必大费；多藏必厚亡。

故知足不辱，知止不殆，可以长久。

名與身孰親	Which is dearer—your reputation or your life?
身與貨孰多	Which is more valuable—your life or your goods?
得與亡孰病	Which is more vulnerable—your gain or your loss?
甚愛必大費	Too much doting leads to big waste;
多藏必厚亡	Too much hoarding leads to great loss.
故知足不辱	Therefore resting content is not humiliating;
知止不殆	Knowing when to stop is not dangerous.
可以長久	For that's the way to last.

COMMENTARY

Laozi's persuasive power is irresistible because he appeals to your self-interest rather than preaches any moral principle. Self-interest is part of nature and is therefore readily acceptable when an argument is made in its name. A moral code, on the other hand, is artificially constructed and, no matter how high-sounding, often goes against the grain of human inclination. Of course self-interest may lead to greed and waste, but by pointing out the hazards of greed and recommending contentment as its alternative, Laozi convincingly makes his point without throwing out the baby with the bathwater. Since greed was a widespread malaise in his time and beyond, Laozi comes back to the issue again and again to recommend the alternative.

....

45

大成若缺，其用不弊。大盈若冲，其用不穷。大直若屈，大巧若拙，大辩
若讷。

静胜躁，寒胜热。清静为天下正。

大成若缺	Great perfection seems incomplete;
其用不弊	Its use never expires.
大盈若冲	Great abundance seems empty;
其用不窮	Its use is inexhaustible.
大直若屈	Great straightness seems crooked;
大巧若拙	Great agility seems awkward;
大辯若訥	Great eloquence seems tongue-tied.
靜勝躁	Stillness overcomes restlessness;
寒勝熱	Cold overcomes heat.
清静爲天下正	Tranquility sets the benchmark for the world.

COMMENTARY ....

Here is another cache of paradoxical sayings in the "A is like B" formula.
The lesson lies in the difference between appearance and reality, between
embellishment and substance. To attain *Dao*, one needs to know the
difference and focus on the substance. The problem is that people too often
look for perfection in appearance at the expense of substance. They crave
opulence instead of true abundance; they go for shortcuts instead of honest
mileage; they pretend adroitness and look down upon true skills; they are
proud of their glib tongue but fail to deliver their message. Laozi attributes

these human frailties to restlessness and excessive heat. The antidote to these is to calm and cool down, for tranquility is the standard *Dao* has set up for the world.

Laozi's call for tranquility stems from his understanding of *wuwei*. It is in the nature of *Dao* to remain soft, still, cool, and tranquil while letting things take their own course. That is the essence of Non-doing.

天下有道，却走马以粪。天下无道，戎马生于郊。

祸莫大于不知足；咎莫大于欲得。故知足之足，常足矣。

天下有道	When the world is governed by *Dao*,
却走馬以糞	War horses are retired to plow the fields.
天下無道	When the world is not governed by *Dao*,
戎馬生於郊	Colts are born on the battlefields.
禍莫大於不知足	No calamity is greater than discontent;
咎莫大於欲得	No mistake is greater than greed.
故知足之足	Therefore it is the contentment of being content
常足矣	That is the everlasting content.

COMMENTARY

The discourse on *Dao* is not just so much abstract metaphysics; it is situated at the heart of the most pressing issue of the day, namely, war and peace. Laozi contrasts vividly the woes of war against the blessings of peace by describing the changing behaviors of horses in different times. He attributes war, the worst human calamity, to human avarice or the absence of content. Once again he urges people to understand the value of contentedness so they can live forever in peace.

The character 糞 (*fèn*) in the second line means "manure" in modern Chinese. Here it means "to plow or till the fields."

不出户，知天下；不窥牖，见天道。其出弥远，其知弥少。

是以圣人不行而知，不见而明，不为而成。

不出户	You need not go outdoors
知天下	To know about the world.
不闚牖	You need not peek through the window
見天道	To understand the Heavenly *Dao*.
其出彌遠	The farther you travel,
其知彌少	The less you know.
是以聖人	That is why the sage
不行而知	Knows without traveling,
不見而明	Understands without seeing,
不爲而成	Achieves without doing.

COMMENTARY

Laozi is positing two approaches to knowledge: to pursue knowledge of the mundane world, which relies on empirical data, and to pursue knowledge of *Dao*, which relies on meditation. Most people go traveling all over the place in a restless attempt to see everything with their own eyes. But for those who wish to understand *Dao*, this is not the right approach because it upsets one's inner tranquility and shuts down the wisdom of the mind. As Laozi puts it, "The farther you travel, the less you know." That is why the sage cuts back on his contacts with the outside world and focuses on his inner vision. As Laozi says in chapter 45, "Stillness overcomes restlessness," and "Tranquility sets the benchmark for the world."

为学日益；为道日损。损之又损，以至于无为。无为而无不为。取天下常以无事，及其有事，不足以取天下。

爲學日益	To pursue learning you increase day by day;
爲道日損	To pursue *Dao* you decrease day by day.
損之又損	Decrease and yet again decrease,
以至於無爲	Till you reach the state of Non-doing.
無爲而無不爲	Do nothing and yet nothing is not done.
取天下常以無事	The world is often won without busying around;
及其有事	When busying around occurs,
不足以取天下	The world cannot be won.

COMMENTARY

The poignancy of this chapter can be better appreciated if you keep in mind Confucius' teachings on learning. The *Analects* famously begins with the statement "Study and practice in good time what you have learned. Isn't that a pleasure?" Confucius also encourages people to "Study, excel and become an elite." Confucius is fostering a culture of incremental learning and active doing. By contrast, Laozi promotes a counterculture that is decremental and quietistic. The goal is for society to return to a state of peaceful Non-doing. To follow Laozi's teaching, however, one needs to stop busying around with things. A busybody can never have the wisdom to govern the world.

49

圣人常无心；以百姓心为心。善者，吾善之；不善者，吾亦善之；德善。信者，吾信之；不信者，吾亦信之；德信。

圣人在天下，歙歙焉。为天下浑其心。百姓皆注其耳目；圣人皆孩之。

聖人常無心	The sage never has a heart and mind of his own;
以百姓心爲心	He takes everyone's heart and mind as his.
善者吾善之	Those who are good I treat with good;
不善者吾亦善之	Those who are not good I also treat with good—
德善	Till good prevails.
信者吾信之	Those who are trustworthy I trust;
不信者吾亦信之	Those who are not trustworthy I also trust—
德信	Till trust prevails.

聖人在天下	The sage rules this world
歙歙焉	Inhaling every breath with caution.
爲天下渾其心	He tries to blur the mind of the world.
百姓皆注其耳目	People all focus on their ears and eyes;
聖人皆孩之	The sage treats them all as children.

COMMENTARY

The word 心 (*xīn*) refers to both the heart and the mind. To say "The sage never has a heart and mind of his own" is like saying "Heaven and Earth are not humane" and "The sage is not humane" in chapter 5. People expect the sage to have a heart and mind that can tell the good and trustworthy from their opposites and act accordingly. But the sage never has a heart and mind that is independent of *Dao*. He treats all humans with goodwill and trust until both eventually prevail. Here we see the character 德 (*dé*) in 德善 (*dé shàn*) and 德信 (*dé xìn*). In many redactions, it appears as 得 (*dé*), which means "to get" or "reach." Based on this reading, I translate the character as "prevail." The first person "I" does not have to refer to Laozi himself. It simply puts the reader in the position of the subject, which in this case is the sage. Such an idiomatic use of the first-person pronoun is still alive in modern Chinese.

Living in this complex world, the sage treats every person and event with extreme caution as if he is inhaling each breath in a gingerly fashion. Indeed, he tries to blur the mind of the world to restore them to the state of innocence. People tend to rely on their subjective observations through their ears and eyes, but he treats them all like children in their infancy.

50

出生入死。生之徒，十有三；死之徒，十有三；人之生，动之于死地，亦十有三。夫何故？以其生生之厚。

盖闻善摄生者，陆行不遇兕虎，入军不被甲兵；兕无所投其角，虎无所用其爪，兵无所容其刃。夫何故？以其无死地。

出生入死	Of all who go from birth to death,
生之徒	Those who live long
十有三	Are three out of ten;
死之徒	Those who die young
十有三	Are three out of ten;
人之生	Those who are alive
動之於死地	But mill around in the field of death—
亦十有三	Are also three out of ten.
夫何故	Now why is that?
以其生生之厚	It is because they take too good care of their lives.
蓋聞善攝生者	I have heard those who know how to preserve themselves
陸行不遇兕虎	Do not encounter rhinos or tigers when traveling on land,
入軍不被甲兵	Do not wear armor when going into battle;
兕無所投其角	That the rhino finds no spot to butt its horn,
虎無所用其爪	That the tiger finds no spot to sink its claws,
兵無所容其刃	That the weapon finds no spot to thrust its blade.
夫何故	Now why is that?
以其無死地	It is because they are not in the field of death.

COMMENTARY ....

Longevity is one of the major concerns of *Daodejing*. As the Lord of the River makes clear in his opening commentaries, the eternal *Dao* is the way to live a natural and long life. Given the high mortality rate of Laozi's time, one third is perhaps about right for those who live relatively long as well as for those who die young. Laozi's interest is in the remaining one third who "are alive but mill around in the field of death." Living in the field of death means living in the shadow of death. These people care so much for their material well-being and sensual pleasures that they make themselves vulnerable and more dead than alive. By contrast, those who know how to nourish their lives stay clear from unwanted substance and unnecessary worries so that they are out of the field of death and invulnerable to harm. They are the ones who have no weak spot on their body or mind open to the attack of wild animals or enemy swords.

51

道生之，德畜之，物形之，势成之。

是以万物莫不尊道而贵德。

道之尊，德之贵，夫莫之命而常自然。

故道生之，德畜之；长之育之；亭之毒之；养之覆之。

生而不有，为而不恃，长而不宰，是谓玄德。

道生之	*Dao* gives birth to them;
德畜之	*De* nurtures them;
物形之	Form shapes them;
勢成之	Circumstances make them.

是以萬物莫不尊道而貴德	That is why all things revere *Dao* and honor *De*.

道之尊	*Dao* is revered,
德之貴	*De* is honored,
夫莫之命而常自然	Because they never give orders but always let things be.

故道生之	Thus *Dao* gives birth to all things,
德畜之	And *De* nurtures them—
長之育之	Raises and cultivates them,
亭之毒之	Mellows and matures them,
養之覆之	Tends and shields them.

生而不有	Birthing but not possessing,
爲而不恃	Getting things done but not taking advantage,

長而不宰　　　　　　　Leading but not dominating—
是謂玄德　　　　　　　This is called the Profound *De*.

COMMENTARY ··

Once again we see in this chapter that *De*, as the emanated One, bears all the powers and qualities of *Dao*. It is *Dao* that is the ultimate source of all life, while *De* does all the work of nurturing, cultivating, and accomplishing on *Dao*'s behalf. Both *Dao* and *De* earn the respect of all things because of their caring but non-possessive attitude. Laozi concludes on an emphatic note that this is what he means by "Profound *De*."

52

....

天下有始，以为天下母。既得其母，以知其子；既知其子，复守其母，没身不殆。

塞其兑，闭其门，终身不勤。开其兑，济其事，终身不救。

见小曰明，守柔曰强。用其光，复归其明，无遗身殃；是为袭常。

天下有始	The world has a beginning;
以爲天下母	That is the mother of the world.
既得其母	Once you get to know the mother,
以知其子	You understand her children.
既知其子	Once you understand the children,
復守其母	You return to the mother—
没身不殆	To the end of your life you will have no peril.
塞其兑	Stop all outlets,
閉其門	Close all doors—
終身不勤	To the end of your life you will be free from hassle.
開其兑	Unplug the outlets,
濟其事	Encourage activities—
終身不救	To the end of your life you will be incorrigible.
見小曰明	Seeing the small is called enlightenment;
守柔曰强	Staying soft is called strength.
用其光	Take advantage of the light,
復歸其明	Return to your enlightenment,
無遺身殃	Bring no more calamity to yourself—
是爲襲常	That is the legacy of eternity.

COMMENTARY ....

As in chapter 1, "Nameless is the beginning of Heaven and Earth; named is the Mother of all things," Laozi is demonstrating the mother-child relationship between *Dao* and all things. To understand the diverse behaviors of all things, one needs first of all to know *Dao*. Once you know *Dao*, you can apply this knowledge to understand all things. When you see *Dao* manifested in all things, you go back to *Dao* and abide by its principles. This is a process of quietly discerning every tiny expression of *Dao* through meditation, not through busy inquiries and active intervention. That is the meaning of stopping the outlets and closing the doors. Laozi expresses the same idea in chapter 47, where he says, "You need not go outdoors to know about the world. You need not peek through the window to understand the Heavenly *Dao*." "Stopping the outlets and closing the doors" also means blocking the access to allurements of greed to focus on one's inner wisdom or enlightenment. That way you can avoid calamities and inherit the legacy of eternity.

53

使我介然有知，行于大道，唯施是畏。大道甚夷，而人好径。朝甚除，田甚芜，仓甚虚；服文彩，带利剑、厌饮食，财货有余；是谓盗夸。非道也哉。

使我介然有知	If I know a little of anything,
行於大道	When I travel on the main road,
唯施是畏	What I fear most is going astray.
大道甚夷	The main road is flat and smooth,
而人好徑	Yet some people prefer the by-paths.
朝甚除	Their palaces are spotlessly clean,
田甚蕪	Their fields lie in waste,
倉甚虛	Their barns quite empty.
服文綵	They wear embroidered satin,
帶利劍	Carry all-penetrating swords,
厭飲食	Indulge in food and drink,
財貨有餘	Luxuriate in wealth and goods.
是謂盜夸	That is *dao* the bandit chief,
非道也哉	Not *Dao* the Main Road.

COMMENTARY

Most received editions and the Mawangdui scripts use the character 民 (*mín*) for 人 (*rén*) in line 5. Though the two words may sometimes be interchangeable, 民 (*mín*) in Laozi's time refers mostly to the lower-class people, whereas 人 (*rén*) is a polite, indirect reference to the rulers. Judging by the present context, those who own palaces, wear satin, and indulge in good life cannot be 民 (*mín*). Hence we follow the emendation of some commentators.

Laozi plays on the homonyms 盗 (*dào*), meaning "robber" or "bandit," and 道 (*dào*), meaning "*Dao*" or "the main road." The pun amounts to a biting satire on those corrupt rulers who rob their subjects in the name of *Dao*.

54

善建者不拔；善抱者不脱，子孫以祭祀不輟。

修之于身，其德乃真；修之于家，其德乃余；修之于鄉，其德乃長；修之于邦，其德乃豐；修之于天下，其德乃普。

故以身觀身，以家觀家，以鄉觀鄉，以邦觀邦，以天下觀天下。吾何以知天下然哉？以此。

善建者不拔	Good builders do not give up;
善抱者不脱	Good holders do not let go;
子孫以祭祀不輟	Lineage worshipers do not quit.

修之於身	Cultivate this in yourself,
其德乃真	And your *De* will be genuine.
修之於家	Cultivate this in your family,
其德乃餘	And your *De* will be plenty.
修之於鄉	Cultivate this in your village,
其德乃長	And your *De* will take the lead.
修之於邦	Cultivate this in your state,
其德乃豐	And your *De* will be abundant.
修之於天下	Cultivate this in the whole world,
其德乃普	And your *De* will be universal.

故以身觀身	Thus through one person you observe all persons;
以家觀家	Through one family you observe all families;
以鄉觀鄉	Through one village you observe all villages;
以邦觀邦	Through one state you observe all states;
以天下觀天下	And through the world you observe the world.
吾何以知天下然哉	How do I know that the world is like this?
以此	That is how.

COMMENTARY ....

The first stanza stresses persistence and endurance, a widely acceptable principle for any form of cultivation. The second and third stanzas throw new light on the meaning and method of *De* cultivation.

To readers who are familiar with the Confucian canon, the two stanzas are reminiscent of the teachings of *The Great Learning*. This classic lays out a road map of moral cultivation starting with the individual person. Here is a partial quotation:

> Wishing to illuminate luminous virtue throughout the world, you would first govern your state. Wishing to govern your state, you would first bring order to your family. Wishing to bring order to your family, you would first cultivate your own person. . . . When the person is cultivated, order is brought to the family. When order is brought to the family, the state is well governed. When the state is well governed, peace is brought to the world. (de Bary and Bloom, 1999, 330–331)

But Laozi does not have such an ambitious agenda for the cultivation of *De*. He wants the aspirant to *De* to concentrate on observing or contemplating the domain he is in at the moment, be it the individual person, family, village, state, or the whole world, one thing at a time. The job is to observe or 觀 (*guān*), not to control. The observer does not harbor any agenda for the next phase, but in the end he comes to understand the whole world. We remember Laozi using the same word 觀 (*guān*) in chapter 1, where he says, "Through eternal Nonbeing, one observes its mystery; through eternal Being, one observes its manifestations." That is the way *one comes* to know *Dao*.

If there is a parallel to Laozi's approach to cultivation, it occurs in the book named after the great thinker and statesman Guanzi 管子 (c. 725–645 BCE). Since we know for certain that the book was not written by Guanzi himself and may date as late as 190 BCE, we cannot call that an influence on Laozi. But this is what the author of *Guanzi* says concerning governance:

> If you govern a village by family standards, the village will not be well governed. If you govern a state by village standards, the state will not be well governed. If you govern the world by state standards, the world will not be well governed. [So] Govern the family by family standards. Govern the village by village standards. Govern the state by state standards. Govern the world by world standards. (See *Guanzi*, book 1, chapter 1)

55

含德之厚，比于赤子。毒虫不螫，猛兽不据，攫鸟不搏。骨弱筋柔而握固。未知牝牡之合而朘作，精之至也。终日号而不嗄，和之至也。

知和曰常，知常曰明。益生曰祥。心使气曰强。物壮则老，是谓不道。不道早已。

含德之厚	One who is well endowed with *De*
比於赤子	May be likened to a newborn infant:
毒蟲不螫	Poisonous insects do not sting him;
猛獸不據	Ferocious animals do not grab him;
攫鳥不搏	Birds of prey do not pounce on him.
骨弱筋柔而握固	Bones weak, tendons soft, yet his grip is firm;
未知牝牡之合而朘作	He knows nothing about sex, yet his penis erects:
精之至也	That is because his essence is in ample supply.
終日號而不嗄	He cries all day but never gets hoarse:
和之至也	That is because he is in perfect harmony.
知和曰常	Understanding harmony means knowing the constant;
知常曰明	Knowing the constant means enlightenment;
益生曰祥	Indulging in good life means ill omen;
心使氣曰強	Letting the mind direct *Qi* means using force.
物壯則老	Things that resort to force age fast.
是謂不道	That is called going against *Dao*.
不道早已	Going against *Dao* brings early demise.

COMMENTARY ....

Laozi says in chapter 10, "Focusing your *Qi* till you reach suppleness, can you be like an infant?" Infancy is the softest, most defenseless, most vulnerable phase of human life. Yet an infant's grip is firm, its energy seems inexhaustible, and its body seems immune to attacks by poisonous or ferocious animals. This power comes from his primordial *Qi* or vital energy. It is self-sufficient and self-renewable. Abusing this vital energy only brings ominous results, and trying to direct it with one's mind only turns its natural power into its opposite: unnatural force. Laozi concludes the chapter with the proverbial warning: Things that resort to force age fast, and premature aging leads to early death. The last three lines are the same as the concluding lines of chapter 30. Since no commentator has taken issue with the repetition, it can only be read as a reiteration.

56

....

知者不言，言者不知。

塞其兑，闭其门，挫其锐，解其纷，和其光，同其尘，是谓玄同。故不可得而亲，不可得而疏；不可得而利，不可得而害；不可得而贵，不可得而贱。故为天下贵。

知者不言	Those who know don't speak;
言者不知	Those who speak don't know.
塞其兑	Stop all outlets,
閉其門	Close all doors,
挫其銳	Blunt the sharpness,
解其紛	Resolve the differences,
和其光	Soften the light,
同其塵	Blend in with the dust—
是謂玄同	That is called Profound Commonality.
故不可得而親	Attaining this, you will not feel favored;
不可得而疏	Attaining this, you will not feel estranged;
不可得而利	Attaining this, you will not seek profits;
不可得而害	Attaining this, you will not do harm;
不可得而貴	Attaining this, you will not become ennobled;
不可得而賤	Attaining this, you will not become debased—
故爲天下貴	That is why the whole world honors such a state.

COMMENTARY ....

The first two lines do not seem to be relevant to the rest of the chapter. They may have been misplaced here by copyists. The character 知 (*zhī*), meaning "know," is also a variant of 智 (*zhi*), meaning "wise." Some ancient versions of *Daodejing* actually use 智. So the first two lines may also be translated as "Those who are wise do not speak; those who speak are not wise."

The first two lines of the second stanza also appear in chapter 52. They too may have been misplaced here by copyists.

Laozi is describing an attainable state which he calls Profound Commonality. "Soften the light" means softening the glare of the light to blur the focus on differences. "Blend in with the dust" implies joining the common people and getting one's hands dirty in a common endeavor. It transcends all considerations of human relations, personal gains, and social status. Notice the repetition of the word 得 (*dé*), which is homonymous with 德 (*dé*).

57

....

以正治国，以奇用兵，以无事取天下。吾何以知其然哉？以此：

天下多忌讳，而民弥贫；人多利器，国家滋昏；人多伎巧，奇物滋起；法令滋彰，盗贼多有。

故圣人云：我无为，而民自化；我好静，而民自正；我无事，而民自富；我无欲，而民自朴。

以正治國	Govern the state by the proper norm,
以奇用兵	Conduct warfare with surprise,
以無事取天下	Win the world without meddling.
吾何以知其然哉	How do I know it is so?
以此	Because of this:
天下多忌諱	The more inhibitions the world has,
而民彌貧	The more impoverished the common people become.
人多利器	The more weapons the ruler has,
國家滋昏	The more disorderly the state becomes.
人多伎巧	The more cunning the ruler uses,
奇物滋起	The more untoward things happen.
法令滋彰	The more laws and decrees are issued,
盜賊多有	The more bandits and thieves come forth.
故聖人云	Therefore the sage says:
我無爲	I do nothing,
而民自化	And the common people change of themselves.
我好靜	I stay still,
而民自正	And the common people get things right for themselves.
我無事	I do not meddle,

而民自富　　　　And the common people make themselves prosperous.
我無欲　　　　　I have no desires,
而民自樸　　　　And the common people keep themselves simple.

COMMENTARY ....

This and the next few chapters all have to do with the application of *wuwei* or Non-doing to governance, which includes both intrastate and interstate affairs in the multistate world of Laozi's time. The characters 正 (*zhèng*) and 奇 (*qí*) form a pair of opposites. Literally 正 (*zhèng*) means "the norm," neither falling short nor going over, tilting neither this way nor that. Doing something just right is the most direct and least costly way. It amounts to "doing nothing." Opposite to 正 (*zhèng*) is 奇 (*qí*), which means "odd," or "strange" or "devious." To be odd may mean going out of the normal way and taking people by surprise. In that sense, oddity can serve a good end. Applied to military affairs, this could be the most efficient way to bring the war to a close with the least cost in human lives. But if too much cunning is employed in running state affairs, unpleasantly odd things may happen, leading to social instability.

As for winning the world, commentators have pointed out that it does not refer to military conquest so much as winning the support of the populace. And the best way to do that is to refrain from any meddling. So the first three lines show different ways of applying Non-doing. Laozi says he comes to these conclusions for good reason.

The second stanza begins with the sentence "The more inhibitions the world has, the more impoverished the common people become." That is what we see in the received version. But instead of "impoverished" or 貧

(*pín*), the recently discovered Guodian text has the character 畔 (*pàn*), a variant of 叛 (*pàn*) meaning "to rebel." Thus the sentence reads, "The more inhibitions the world has, the more rebellious the common people become," which seems to make better sense. The whole stanza gives compelling evidence of the negative effect of repressive measures. Note the character 人 (*rén*) (people) appears twice in this sentence to refer to the ruler.

The third stanza drives home the benefits of Non-doing or 無爲 (*wú wéi*) and non-meddling or 無事 (*wú shì*). It reminds us of chapter 17, where Laozi describes the best ruler as one who practices Non-doing and lets people get things done for themselves.

58

其政闷闷，其民淳淳；其政察察，其民缺缺。祸兮，福之所倚；福兮，祸之所伏。孰知其极？其无正也。正复为奇，善复为妖。人之迷，其日固久。

是以圣人方而不割，廉而不刿，直而不肆，光而不耀。

其政悶悶	When government policy is general and vague,
其民淳淳	The common people are honest and simple;
其政察察	When government policy is meticulous and severe,
其民缺缺	The common people become wily and crafty.
禍兮福之所倚	Misfortune is what fortune leans on;
福兮禍之所伏	Fortune is what misfortune hides under.
孰知其極	Who knows the boundary?
其無正也	There is no absolute standard.
正復爲奇	Right can turn into wrong;
善復爲妖	Good can turn into evil.
人之迷	People have been puzzled
其日固久	For a very long time.
是以聖人	Therefore the sage is
方而不割	Square but does not cut,
廉而不劌	Incisive but does not hurt,
直而不肆	Direct but not unrestrained
光而不耀	Brilliant but not glaring.

COMMENTARY ···

All things in this world are changeable and unpredictable. So the best policy of a ruler is to be vague and tolerant while the common people are kept in their unspoiled state of honesty and simplicity.

It is in this context that we find the famous proverb "Misfortune is what fortune leans on; fortune is what misfortune hides under," which leads to a later, equally popular legend of the Han dynasty. The story goes like this: An old man living on the northern border lost his beloved horse one day, and all his neighbors came to express their sympathy. The old man said, "Oh, you never know if this is real misfortune." A couple of days later the horse returned from across the border with an even more beautiful horse, and his neighbors came to congratulate the old man. All he said was, "Oh, you never know if this is real good fortune." His son saw the new horse and took it out for a ride. Unfortunately he had a fall and broke his leg. The neighbors again came to express sympathy, but the old man again said, "Oh, you never know if this is real misfortune." Sure enough, a few days later, the army recruiters came to summon the son to serve in war. Seeing his broken leg, the officer yielded and left. You know how the old man responded. (See *Huai Nan Zi*, chapter 18.)

Most people are puzzled why things do not turn out as they predicted. But Laozi asks, "Who knows the boundary?" By that he means, "Who knows where one ends and the other begins?" When Laozi uses the word 人 (*rén*) or people, he is referring to the average rulers of the feudal states or members of the ruling circles. Their role model is the legendary 聖人 (*shèng rén*) or "sage ruler." These people are supposed to be educated, but they have been puzzled for a long time. Understanding this conundrum, the sage chooses to be general and vague in his governance instead of coming down hard on one side or the other.

59

治人事天，莫若嗇。

夫唯嗇，是谓早服；早服谓之重积德；重积德则无不克；无不克则莫知其极；
莫知其极，可以有国；有国之母，可以长久；是谓深根固柢，长生久视之道。

治人事天	In governing people and serving Heaven,
莫若嗇	There is nothing like conservation.
夫唯嗇	For to conserve
是謂早服	Means to be prepared early.
早服謂之重積德	To be prepared early means ample accumulation of *De*.
重積德則無不克	Ample accumulation of *De* means being invincible.
無不克則莫知其極	An invincible power knows no limit.
莫知其極可以有國	With power that knows no limit, one can govern the state.
有國之母可以長久	With the Mother as the guardian, the state can last long.
是謂深根固柢	That is called deep roots and solid foundation.
長生久視之道	And that is the way to long life and lasting existence.

COMMENTARY

The character 嗇 (*sè*) in modern Chinese generally denotes miserliness. But Laozi uses it in a positive sense to refer to conserving one's vital energy in proportion to one's *De* credits. Such accumulation prepares the ruler from an early age to govern and care for his state. The "Mother" is the Mother of all things, that is, *Dao*. According to the Lord of the River's commentaries, taking Mother *Dao* as one's guardian means preserving the essence of one's vital energy so that his state as well as his own life can last long.

60

治大国，若烹小鲜。

以道莅天下，其鬼不神；非其鬼不神，其神不伤人；非其神不伤人，圣人亦不伤人。夫两不相伤，故德交归焉。

治大國	Governing a large state
若烹小鮮	Is like cooking a small fish.
以道莅天下	When *Dao* prevails over the world,
其鬼不神	The demons lose their spiritual power.
非其鬼不神	Not only do demons lose their spiritual power,
其神不傷人	The spirits do not hurt people.
非其神不傷人	Not only do spirits not hurt people,
聖人亦不傷人	The sage does not hurt people either.
夫兩不相傷	Because neither party hurts,
故德交歸焉	*De* is able to converge and return to its origin.

COMMENTARY

"Cooking a small fish," as the Lord of the River explains in his commentaries, requires special care. Because the fish is small, you are not supposed to remove its entrails and scales in preparation or stir it when cooking lest you turn it into mush. Likewise, when governing a large state, the ruler should not disturb its people but leave them in peace and let *Dao* prevail. When *Dao* prevails, both the spiritual and the human world are at peace and *De* is able to complete its work and return to its origin to rest.

61

大邦者下流，天下之牝，天下之交也。牝常以静胜牡，以静为下。

故大邦以下小邦，则取小邦。小邦以下大邦，则取大邦。故或下以取，或下而取，大邦不过欲兼畜人，小邦不过欲入事人。夫两者各得所欲，大者宜为下。

大邦者下流	The big states lie on the lower reaches of the rivers,
天下之牝	These are places for the female of the world,
天下之交也	Places where the world converges.
牝常以静勝牡	The female invariably overcomes the male by being still,
以静爲下	And in stillness she takes the lower position.
故大邦以下小邦	So if a big state stays below a small state,
則取小邦	It wins over the small state.
小邦以下大邦	If a small state stays below a big state,
則取大邦	It wins over the big state.
故或下以取	Whether they stay below in order to win,
或下而取	Or whether they stay below and win,
大邦不過欲兼畜人	All the big state wants is to incorporate the other;
小邦不過欲入事人	All the small state wants is to partner with the other.
夫兩者各得所欲	Since both can get what they want,
大者宜爲下	It is better for the bigger state to take the lower position.

COMMENTARY

Just as Laozi applies *wuwei* or Non-doing to domestic governance of feudal states, he applies the same principle to the external affairs between these states. Here he sees a win-win situation for states both big and small as long as they are willing to take the lowly and humble position. The Chinese character for that is 下 (*xià*), which can mean either "below" or "underneath." Laozi is thinking about both the geographical vantage point of being on the lower reaches of the big rivers and the sexual position of the female lying underneath, thereby overcoming the male. Because he takes this feminist approach, he does not talk about "conquering" a state but "winning over" a state, be it big or small.

62

道者万物之奥。善人之宝，不善人之所保。

美言可以市尊，美行可以加人。人之不善，何弃之有？故立天子，置三公，虽有拱璧以先驷马，不如坐进此道。

古之所以贵此道者何？不曰，求以得，有罪以免邪？故为天下贵。

道者萬物之奧	*Dao* is the sanctuary for all.
善人之寶	It is a treasure for the good,
不善人之所保	And a warranty for the not so good.
美言可以市尊	Beautiful words may win people's respect;
美行可以加人	Beautiful deeds may earn people's admiration.
人之不善	So even if a person is not so good,
何棄之有	Why abandon him?
故立天子	Therefore, when the Son of Heaven is enthroned
置三公	And the Three Elders are installed,
雖有拱璧	Though you may present a jade disc as tribute,
以先駟馬	Followed by a carriage of four,
不如坐進此道	It is better to just sit and admonish with this teaching.
古之所以貴此道者何	Why did the ancients value this teaching?
不曰	Has it not been said,
求以得	"If you seek, you will receive,
有罪以免邪	And if you are guilty, you will be spared?"
故爲天下貴	That is why all under Heaven value this teaching.

COMMENTARY ....

Under the umbrella of the all-embracing *Dao*, everything, both the good and not good, has its use. Even beautiful words and deeds, though not always sincere, may have their face value. Further, *Dao* provides a recourse for the not so good to seek their fortune and be spared of punishment for their guilt. That is why Laozi calls *Dao* the sanctuary for all and the warranty for the not so good. In the spirit of this teaching, I have translated 不善 (*bù shàn*) not literally as "not good" but "not so good."

"The Son of Heaven" is the title for the head of the Zhou dynasty (1046–221 BCE). "The Three Elders" refers to *Taishi*, *Taifu*, and *Taibao*, the three highest-ranking officials under the head.

63

为无为，事无事，味无味。

大小多少，图难于其易，为大于其细。天下难事，必作于易；天下大事，必作于细。是以，圣人终不为大，故能成其大。

夫轻诺必寡信，多易必多难。是以，圣人犹难之，故终无难矣。

爲無爲	Do without doing,
事無事	Serve without meddling,
味無味	Savor the savorless.

大小多少	Big or small, many or few,
圖難於其易	Tackle the difficult when it is easy;
爲大於其細	Attack the big when it is small.
天下難事	All difficulties under Heaven
必作於易	Begin with the easy;
天下大事	All big things under Heaven
必作於細	Begin with the small.
是以	Therefore,
聖人終不爲大	The sage never tries to tackle the big
故能成其大	And always accomplishes the big.

夫輕諾必寡信	For making rash promises impairs credibility;
多易必多難	Taking things too easy causes too many difficulties.
是以	Therefore,
聖人猶難之	The sage treats everything as difficult
故終無難矣	And ends up with no difficulty.

COMMENTARY ....

This is perhaps the most lucid and most down-to-earth explanation of *wuwei* or Non-doing for everyday application. The essence of it is summed up in the lines "Tackle the difficult when it is easy; attack the big when it is small." But that is not all. Laozi adds in the second stanza, which says that one has to treat what is easy as if it was difficult. If you are negligent with things that seem small and easy, they can accumulate into a big pile of difficulties. It all sounds like common sense, but we all need Laozi's timely admonition.

Applying the above principle to governance, Laozi sounds a stern warning against making rash promises. In contrast, he invokes the sage ruler, who never treats little things lightly and always accomplishes big.

The line "Big or small, many or few" consists of four of the simplest characters in Chinese: 大 (*dà*), 小 (*xiǎo*), 多 (*duō*), and 少 (*shǎo*). The intriguing part lies in putting these characters into meaningful syntax. At the literal level, it could just mean "no matter whether it's big or small, many or few." But the flexible grammar of classical Chinese permits adjectives to be used as verbs or nouns and vice versa so that one could "small" or minimize the big and "few" or reduce the many. One could also "big" or maximize the small and "many" or multiply the few. Thus the same four characters could be translated as "Treat as big the small; treat as many the few" or "Reduce the big to the small, the many to the few." Actually all these alternative translations are possible in elucidating the principle of Non-doing.

64

其安易持；其未兆易谋；其脆易泮；其微易散。为之于未有，治之于未乱。

合抱之木，生于毫末；九层之台，起于累土；千里之行，始于足下。

为者败之，执者失之。是以圣人无为故无败；无执故无失。

民之从事，常于几成而败之。慎终如始，则无败事。

是以圣人欲不欲，不贵难得之货；学不学，复众人之所过，以辅万物之自然而不敢为。

其安易持	It is easy to manage when the situation is stable;
其未兆易謀	Easy to plan ahead before things look ominous;
其脆易泮	Easy to crack when things are fragile;
其微易散	Easy to scatter when things are little.
爲之於未有	Act before something happens;
治之於未亂	Take control before there is turmoil.
合抱之木	A tree with the girth of a man's embrace
生於毫末	Grows out of a tiny shoot.
九層之臺	A terrace nine stories high
起於累土	Rises from a basket of dirt.
千里之行	The journey of a thousand *li*
始於足下	Begins under your feet.
爲者敗之	Those who act fail;
執者失之	Those who hold lose.
是以聖人無爲故無敗	That is why the sage does not act and so does not fail;
無執故無失	He holds on to nothing and so has nothing to lose.

民之從事	People doing business
常於幾成而敗之	Often fail on the brink of success.
慎終如始	Take caution at the end as at the beginning,
則無敗事	And there will be no failed business.

是以聖人欲不欲	That is why the sage desires what no one else desires,
不貴難得之貨	Sets no store by rare goods,
學不學	Studies what no one else studies,
復眾人之所過	And balances off the excesses of the multitude.
以輔萬物之自然而	He aids all things as they grow without taking over.
不敢為	

COMMENTARY

The second stanza contains three classic metaphors, the last of which has by now become a proverb of world renown: "The journey of a thousand *li* begins under your feet." For English readers it would be more idiomatic to replace the Chinese measurement *li* with "mile." One *li* in today's scale equals 0.311 of a mile. I keep the Chinese unit for the sake of authenticity. By the same token, I use the more literal translation of 足下 (*zú xià*) as "under your feet" although the alternative may read better as an English proverb: "The journey of a thousand miles begins with the first step."

Judging by its content and its placement in the Guodian script, the chapter should most likely be divided into two, with the first ending with "under your feet." We keep it as it is in accordance with the received version since thematically it still hangs together as an elaboration of the principle of Non-doing in the wake of the previous chapter.

65

古之善为道者，非以明民，将以愚之。

民之难治，以其智多。故以智治国，国之贼；不以智治国，国之福。

知此两者亦稽式。常知稽式，是谓玄德。玄德深矣，远矣，与物反矣，然后乃至大顺。

古之善爲道者	In ancient times those who were good at *Dao*
非以明民	Did not use it to enlighten the common people
將以愚之	But to keep them in ignorance.
民之難治	The common people are hard to control
以其智多	Because they have too much intelligence.
故以智治國	Therefore, to govern a state with intelligence
國之賊	Is a woe to the state;
不以智治國	To govern a state with no recourse to intelligence
國之福	Is a blessing to the state.
知此兩者亦稽式	Be aware that these two are different models.
常知稽式	Constant awareness of these models
是謂玄德	Is called Profound *De*.
玄德深矣	Profound *De* is indeed deep;
遠矣	It travels far,
與物反矣	Returns with all things,
然後乃至大順	And eventually reaches Great Conformity.

COMMENTARY ....

Laozi has been blamed for the notorious political doctrine of keeping the people in ignorance, a doctrine that has been the cornerstone of millennia of authoritarian rule by emperors and others. But if that was all that Laozi meant, he would not call it "Profound *De*." In Daoist terms, to "enlighten" people means to stir up people's desire to know and clog their minds with unwanted knowledge. To keep people in "ignorance," on the other hand, means keeping people in their simple, innocent state. To Laozi, "ignorance" (愚 *yú*) is not a derogatory word. He speaks of his own "fool's heart" in chapter 20 and claims that when everything seems crystal clear to ordinary people he alone is dull and dumb. That is the state of mind he wants his people to retain.

Laozi's statement that Profound *De* travels far and returns with all things reiterates what he says in chapter 25 about *Dao* going far and returning in a ceaseless cycle. When *De* returns to *Dao*, it reaches the state of ultimate conformity with what the Lord of the River calls "the Heavenly principles."

66

江海之所以能为百谷王者，以其善下之，故能为百谷王。

是以圣人欲上民，必以言下之；欲先民，必以身后之。

是以圣人处上而民不重，处前而民不害。是以天下乐推而不厌。以其不争，故天下莫能与之争。

江海之所以能爲百谷 王者 — Rivers and seas are the kings of all waters

以其善下之 — Because they love to stay in lowly places.

故能爲百谷王 — That is why they are the kings of all waters.

是以聖人欲上民 — Thus, if the sage wants to lead from the top,

必以言下之 — He must promise to place himself at the bottom.

欲先民 — If he wishes to lead from the front,

必以身後之 — He must place himself in the back.

是以聖人處上而民不重 — In this way, the sage is placed at the top and yet the common people do not feel the weight;

處前而民不害 — He is placed in front and yet the common people do not feel any threat.

是以天下樂推而不厭 — Thus the whole world gladly supports him and never gets tired.

以其不爭 — Just because he does not contend,

故天下莫能與之爭 — No one in this world can contend with him.

COMMENTARY ....

"Kings of all waters" is a free translation of 百谷王 (*bǎi gǔ wáng*), literally "the kings of a hundred ravines." "A hundred" or 百 (*bǎi*) is a plural indicator like "ten thousand" or 萬 (*wàn*) in "ten thousand things" or 萬物 (*wàn wù*). "Ravines" are tributaries to the rivers and seas. The character 王 (*wǎng*) for "king," according to a Han dynasty dictionary, may also refer to what the world yearns to rally around.

67

天下皆谓我大，大而不肖。夫唯不肖，故能大。若肖，久矣其细也。

我有三宝，持而保之。一曰慈，二曰俭，三曰不敢为天下先。

慈故能勇；俭故能广；不敢为天下先，故能成器长。

今舍慈且勇；舍俭且广；舍后且先；死矣。

夫慈，以战则胜，以守则固。天将救之，以慈卫之。

天下皆謂我大	Everyone says I am great,
大而不肖	Great but not talented.
夫唯不肖	Just because I am not talented,
故能大	I am able to be great.
若肖	If I were talented,
久矣其細也	I would have long become small.
我有三寶	I have three treasures,
持而保之	Which I hold dear.
一曰慈	The first is compassion,
二曰儉	The second is frugality,
三曰不敢爲天下先	And the third is refraining from being ahead of the world.
慈故能勇	Compassionate, therefore courageous;
儉故能廣	Frugal, therefore abundant;
不敢爲天下先	Refraining from being ahead of the world,
故能成器長	Therefore serving as the head of all servants.

今舍慈且勇   Nowadays people abandon compassion to seek courage;
舍儉且廣   Abandon frugality to seek abundance;
舍後且先   Abandon the back to seek the front—
死矣   That is a dead end.

夫慈   For compassion
以戰則勝   Brings victory in battle
以守則固   And solidity in defense.
天將救之   Whoever Heaven sets out to rescue,
以慈衛之   Compassion comes to protect.

COMMENTARY

The first stanza seems irrelevant to the rest of this chapter, which is about "compassion" and so forth. It may have been misplaced from an unidentified chapter by copyists or redactors. But since the stanza does exist in the Mawangdui silk scripts as well as the received version, we may as well keep it where it is.

Laozi uses the first person 我 (*wǒ*) or "I" to refer to *Dao* or the Daoist sage. My translation of 不肖 (*bù xiào*) as "not talented" is based on the Lord of the River's commentaries to the effect that the sage "pretends to be foolish and untalented." The phrase could also mean "not resembling," which explains why some commentators and translators think that *Dao* is so great that it bears no specific resemblance to anything concrete. That makes sense too.

Of the three treasures that Laozi holds dear, he lists compassion as number one. The character for "compassion" or 慈 (*cí*) is composed of two parts, 兹 (*zī*) at the top, meaning "this," and 心 (*xīn*) at the bottom, meaning "heart." From this character we see "compassion" means the ability to feel with one's heart what others may feel. When a mother sees someone else's child on the verge of falling into a well, she would rush over to save the child as if it was her own darling baby. Laozi believes we are all capable of such shared feeling. With that capacity we would have the courage not only to defend and save our own people, but also to feel for our enemies and bring any conflict to an early and peaceful end. Unfortunately, Laozi finds in his own time that people too often forget about compassion and look for brutal valor to achieve military exploits. That, he thinks, spells sure death.

Laozi cherishes "frugality" as his second treasure. The character he uses here is 儉 (*jiǎn*), which is synonymous with 嗇 (*sè*) in chapter 59.

68

善为士者，不武；善战者，不怒；善胜敌者，不与；善用人者，为之下。是谓不争之德，是谓用人，是谓配天，古之极也。

善爲士者	A good soldier
不武	Does not use mayhem.
善戰者	A good warrior
不怒	Does not show anger.
善勝敵者	A good winner
不與	Does not contest.
善用人者	A good employer
爲之下	Remains humble.
是謂不爭之德	That is called the virtue of non-contention;
是謂用人	It is also called knowing how to use people,
是謂配天	And being worthy of Heaven.
古之極也	It was the ultimate principle of ancient times.

COMMENTARY

In the military, 士 (*shi*) is a soldier. In civil service, a *shi* is an official scholar. There are other uses of the term depending on the context.

Again Laozi uses the word 下 (*xià*) or "low," which I translate as "humble," to describe the attitude of a sage ruler.

69

用兵有言：吾不敢为主，而为客；不敢进寸、而退尺。是谓行无行；攘无臂；扔无敌；执无兵。

祸莫大于轻敌，轻敌几丧吾宝。

故抗兵相若，哀者胜矣。

用兵有言	The military has a saying:
吾不敢爲主	I do not dare to play host,
而爲客	Much rather play guest;
不敢進寸	I do not dare to advance an inch,
而退尺	Much rather retreat a foot.
是謂行無行	This is called marching without formation,
攘無臂	Flexing muscles without raising an arm,
扔無敵	Facing up without confronting the enemy,
執無兵	Grasping firmly without holding weapons.
禍莫大於輕敵	No disaster is bigger than taking the enemy lightly;
輕敵幾喪吾寶	Taking the enemy lightly almost cost me my treasures.
故抗兵相若	When two armies of equal strength confront,
哀者勝矣	The one in grief wins.

COMMENTARY

The whole idea of playing guest rather than host and retreating a foot rather than advancing an inch sounds like an old trick in military maneuvers. Laozi uses it as an example of one's reluctance to start a war by refusing to make the first move and fire the first shot. It is also a concrete example of how to apply the three treasures of compassion, frugality, and not placing oneself ahead of the world.

"Taking the enemy lightly" is the literal translation of 轻敌 (*qīng dí*). Some translations say "underestimate the enemy." To Laozi, taking the enemy lightly means taking war lightly, taking human lives lightly. When that happens, the three treasures are in jeopardy. On the other hand, if one goes into battle out of self-defense, he does so with compassion and grief at the loss of lives. History has proven such an army is more likely to win.

70

···

吾言甚易知，甚易行。天下莫能知，莫能行。

言有宗，事有君。夫唯无知，是以不我知。

知我者希，则我者贵。是以圣人被褐而怀玉。

吾言甚易知	My words are very easy to understand,
甚易行	And very easy to practice.
天下莫能知	Yet the world cannot understand,
莫能行	And cannot practice.
言有宗	My words have their point,
事有君	My deeds have their grounds.
夫唯無知	But just because they are ignorant
是以不我知	They cannot understand me.
知我者希	Those who understand me are few,
則我者貴	Those who follow my rules are rare.
是以聖人被褐而懷玉	That is why the sage wears coarse linen and holds his jade next to his skin.

COMMENTARY ··

In chapter 20 and elsewhere Laozi prides himself on being the only dullard while everyone else seems sharp and shrewd. We know that has to be read paradoxically. Here the sage is saying his words are very easy to understand and practice but the world doesn't understand him. That too has to be read paradoxically. Laozi is lamenting the fact that too few people understand his teachings and put them into practice. People tend to take him at his coarse face value and overlook the real treasure he embodies.

71

....

知不知，尚矣；不知知，病也。聖人不病，以其病病。夫唯病病，是以不病。

知不知	To know one does not know
尚矣	Is the best;
不知知	To not know but claim one knows
病也	Is sickness.
聖人不病	The sage is not sick
以其病病	Because he sees sickness as sickness.
夫唯病病	Only when one sees sickness as sickness
是以不病	Can one be not sick.

COMMENTARY ....

If you take a quick look at the Chinese text, you will find it hinges mostly on three characters: 知 (*zhī*) (know), 不 (*bù*) (not), and 病 (*bìng*) (sick). Taking advantage of the flexibility of Chinese syntax, Laozi plays on these three characters to generate one of the most succinct texts and most important lessons of all time. English, because of the constraints of its own grammar, can only approximate the original with the help of additional words like "claim" and "see" and functional words like articles and pronouns. Even so, it is impossible to convey the complexity with a single-dimensional translation. Take the first line, for example. On the literal level, "To know one does not know" suggests simple honesty when one is confronted with something he does not know and has to admit ignorance. But on the deeper level, the same line can also be translated as "To know yet still think one does not know." That suggests a greater awareness of one's fundamental limitations as a human being based on one's spiritual consciousness. The word for "sickness" can also refer to a problem or flaw unrelated to biological health. The word can be used as a noun (sickness, disease, etc.), adjective (sick, ill, etc.), or verb (consider or see something as sickness). Like Laozi, Confucius advocates honesty as the best policy in a similar statement in which he juggles with the characters 知 (zhī) (know) and 不 (bù) (not). It goes in Chinese, "知之爲知之，不知爲不知，是知也。" Translated in English it is, "If you know, you know. If you don't know, you don't know. That is wisdom" (Analects, 2.17). By the way, Confucius uses the last 知 (zhī) as an alternative character for 智 (zhī) meaning "wisdom," a practice Laozi also adopts in other chapters. It seems a common phenomenon that great thinkers are also great linguists or even punsters.

72

民不畏威，则大威至。

无狎其所居，无厌其所生。夫唯不厌，是以不厌。

是以圣人自知不自见；自爱不自贵。故去彼取此。

民不畏威	When the common people no longer fear terror,
則大威至	A great terror is imminent.
無狎其所居	Do not constrict their living space;
無厭其所生	Do not oppress their livelihood.
夫唯不厭	Only when there is no oppression,
是以不厭	Will people not feel tired of living.
是以聖人自知不自見	Therefore the sage knows his own worth and does not exhibit himself.
自愛不自貴	He loves himself but does not promote himself.
故去彼取此	Thus he rejects one and prefers the other.

COMMENTARY

Laozi seems to be addressing a grave social crisis in his time when people can no longer tolerate the extreme oppression of a tyrannical ruler. He does so by playing on two characters. The first is 威 (*wēi*) or "terror." He uses it to mean both the rule of terror by an unrestrained tyrant and the terror of mass revolt that erupts in response. The second character is 厭, which may stand for the character 壓 (*yā*), meaning "oppression." But the same character 厭 (*yàn*) means "tired of" or "fed up with." Some commentators think Laozi is saying, "Only when there is no oppression will people not get tired of the ruler." But in the present context, "not get tired" can also mean "not get tired of living." In either case Laozi is deeply concerned with the imminent danger of a major upheaval. Once again he invokes the exemplar of the sage ruler. If a ruler follows the ways of *Dao*, practices Non-doing, and maintains his humility, he is a sage and his rule may be peaceful and lasting. But if he is preoccupied with self-aggrandizement, he becomes increasingly oppressive and the consequences could be disastrous. That is how Laozi links his social concerns with his Daoist worldview.

73

勇于敢则杀；勇于不敢则活。此两者，或利或害。天之所恶，孰知其故？

天之道，不争而善胜，不言而善应，不召而自来，澶然而善谋。天网恢恢，疏而不失。

勇於敢則殺	Daring to be bold means death;
勇於不敢則活	Daring to be not bold means life.
此兩者	Of the two,
或利或害	One seems beneficial and the other harmful.
天之所惡	Whichever Heaven disapproves,
孰知其故	Who knows why?
天之道	The *Dao* of Heaven
不爭而善勝	Does not contend and yet knows how to win;
不言而善應	Does not speak and yet knows how to respond;
不召而自來	Does not wait to be summoned but just shows up.
繟然而善謀	It seems at ease and yet plans well.
天網恢恢	The net of Heaven spreads far and wide;
疏而不失	It seems slack and yet nothing slips through.

COMMENTARY

People generally extol the courage of choosing to be bold as it often runs the risk of death. But the vain glory of boldness is so prevalent that choosing not to be bold would take the same amount of courage as choosing to be bold. One can easily see which kind of courage Laozi prefers. From the point of view of *Dao*, the one that means life is beneficial, while the other, which means death, is harmful. But Laozi does not see things in such a black-and-white way. The stanza ends with a question as to the exact reason why *Dao* disapproves one and not the other. The question itself seems puzzling unless we read the line "one seems beneficial and the other harmful" differently. Can the Chinese 或利或害 (*huò lì huò hài*) be read as "Is one beneficial and the other harmful?" If so, it means that there are pros and cons to either choice. That could be a more interesting way of reading because it leaves us with some degrees of uncertainty that matches the question "Whichever Heaven disapproves, who knows why?" It presents us with an image of a Laozi who does not have all the answers.

The last two lines have become a household proverb to the Chinese, often used in a legalistic sense to suggest that no fugitive can escape the mesh of law. But Laozi is talking about the Non-doing power of *Dao* that does not act but gets everything done that needs to be done.

74

民不畏死，奈何以死惧之？若使民常畏死，而为奇者，吾将得而杀之，孰敢？

常有司杀者杀。夫代司杀者杀，是谓代大匠斵。夫代大匠斵者，希有不伤其手矣。

民不畏死	If the common people do not fear death,
奈何以死懼之	Why scare them with death?
若使民常畏死	If you can make them constantly fear death,
而爲奇者	And there are still those who commit evil,
吾將得而殺之	We could then arrest them and put them to death.
孰敢	Who would dare?
常有司殺者殺	Killing is normally the job of the executioner.
夫代司殺者殺	To substitute the executioner to do the killing
是謂代大匠斵	Is like chopping wood in place of the master woodcutter.
夫代大匠斵者	For if you chop wood in place of the master woodcutter,
希有不傷其手矣	It would hardly be possible if you did not injure your hand.

COMMENTARY

The first two lines have acquired proverbial status often cited to extol the fearless spirit of people in revolt in the face of oppression. But if we place the entire stanza side by side with chapter 72, we find a clear echo of the same theme. In fact, the first lines of both chapters almost have the same wording: 民不畏威 (*mín bù wèi wēi*) (people, not, fear, terror) and 民不畏死 (*mín bù wèi sǐ*) (people, not, fear, death). If oppression is so severe and life is so hard for the common people that they no longer think life is worth living, what follows is desperation and social turmoil. The solution for the ruler is to allow people to live a decent life so that they will still love life and live in fear of forfeiting it. In other words, fearlessness against death is not necessarily a good thing, and what sounds like a revolutionary slogan turns out to be a misprision of meaning.

The second stanza strikes a different note. While Laozi acknowledges that killing those who commit evil could be justifiable when the majority of the people choose to live a peaceful life, he hastens to add that killing is the job of the executioner. He probably has in mind the grand executioner who controls the life and death of all beings, that is, *Dao*. If the ruler presumptuously does the killing on behalf of the executioner, he is going to hurt himself, just like the unprofessional wood chopper who does the chopping in place of the master. A fair warning against those bloodthirsty rulers!

75

民之饥，以其上食税之多，是以饥。

民之难治，以其上之有为，是以难治。

民之轻死，以其上求生之厚，是以轻死。

夫唯无以生为者，是贤于贵生。

民之饑	The common people are hungry
以其上食税之多	Because those above levy too many taxes.
是以饑	That is why they are hungry.
民之難治	The common people are hard to govern
以其上之有爲	Because those above do too much.
是以難治	That is why they are hard to govern.
民之輕死	The common people take death lightly
以其上求生之厚	Because those above care too much for their own life.
是以輕死	That is why they take death lightly.
夫唯無以生爲者	For those who do not do too much for their own life
是賢於貴生	Are wiser than those who seek luxurious life.

COMMENTARY ....

This chapter hits the nail on the head for chapters 72 and 74, the three forming a trio. Here Laozi sees a correlation between the good life of the rulers at the top and the poverty and hunger of the common people below. As poverty and hunger lead to desperation, desperation leads to unrest. What Laozi prescribes for the ruler is to give up his insatiable desire for luxurious life and show greater care for the well-being of the common people.

76

人之生也柔弱，其死也坚强。草木之生也柔脆，其死也枯槁。故坚强者死之徒，柔弱者生之徒。是以兵强则灭，木强则折。坚强处下，柔弱处上。

人之生也柔弱	When alive humans are soft and weak;
其死也堅强	When dead they are hard and stiff.
草木之生也柔脆	Grass and trees are soft and fresh when alive;
其死也枯槁	When dead they dry up and wither away.
故	Thus
堅强者死之徒	That which is hard and stiff belongs to the dead;
柔弱者生之徒	That which is soft and weak belongs to the living.
是以	That is why
兵强則滅	A strong but stiff army is bound to lose;
木强則折	A strong but stiff tree is bound to break.
堅强處下	The hard and stiff are inferior;
柔弱處上	The soft and weak are superior.

COMMENTARY

In no uncertain terms Laozi topples the popular belief that the strong is always the winner and the weak is always the loser. The examples he uses to make his point come from his close observation of natural phenomena. The key word we have to deal with is 堅强 (*jiān qiáng*). The literal meaning of 堅 (*jiān*) is quite straightforward: it is simply "hard" in the sense of "hard to break." The character 强 has two pronunciations, *qiáng* and *jiàng*, representing two related words. Pronounced *qiáng*, it means "strong," "strength" or "strengthen." As *jiàng*, however, it means "stiff" and "inflexible." If we take 堅强 (*jiān qiáng*) as one word as in modern Chinese, it denotes 100 percent positive quality of resilience. But if we take the characters apart and go to their original meanings, then the connotation is no longer all that positive. Once again Laozi proves himself a shrewd observer and a masterful linguist.

77

天之道，其犹张弓与？高者抑之，下者举之；有余者损之，不足者补之。

天之道，损有余而补不足。人之道，则不然，损不足以奉有余。孰能有余以奉天下？唯有道者。

是以圣人为而不恃，功成而不处，其不欲见贤。

天之道	The way of Heaven—
其猶張弓與	Isn't it like shooting with a bow?
高者抑之	If it is aimed too high, you lower it;
下者舉之	If it is aimed too low, you raise it.
有餘者損之	If you use too much force, you reduce it;
不足者補之	If you use insufficient force, you increase it.
天之道	So the way of Heaven
損有餘而補不足	Is to take from the wealthy to supply the needy.
人之道則不然	The way of Man, on the other hand, is different.
損不足以奉有餘	It takes from the needy to enrich the wealthy.
孰能有餘以奉天下	Who can give his wealth to enrich the world?
唯有道者	Only those who have attained *Dao*.
是以聖人爲而不恃	That is why the sage gets things done but never takes advantage,
功成而不處	Accomplishes his work but claims no credit—
其不欲見賢	He simply does not wish to display his excellence.

COMMENTARY ....

Laozi is making a strong statement against human greed and injustice by contrasting the way of Heaven, which takes from the rich to aid the poor, with the way of Man, which robs the poor to satisfy the rich. It shows once more Laozi's deep concern for the social ills of his time. The good news is that there are some like the sage who have attained *Dao* and follow the way of Heaven.

78

天下莫柔弱于水，而攻坚强者莫之能胜，以其无以易之。

弱之胜强，柔之胜刚，天下莫不知，莫能行。

是以圣人云，受国之垢，是谓社稷主；受国不祥，是为天下王。

正言若反。

天下莫柔弱於水	Nothing in this world is softer than water,
而攻堅强者莫之能勝	Yet nothing can better attack the strong than water,
以其無以易之	For nothing can replace it.
弱之勝强	That the weak can subdue the strong
柔之勝剛	And the soft can subdue the tough
天下莫不知	No one in this world does not know,
莫能行	Yet no one can put it into practice.
是以聖人云	That is why the sage says,
受國之垢	He who takes on the disgrace of the state
是謂社稷主	Should be called the leader of society;
受國不祥	He who takes on the calamity of the state
是爲天下王	Should be the king of the world.
正言若反	A truthful statement sounds like its opposite.

COMMENTARY ....

Chinese readers can all cite the proverb 滴水穿石 (*dī shuǐ chuān shí*), "dripping water can penetrate a rock," as testimony to the power of water. Unfortunately, as Laozi puts it, no one does not know this truth, yet no one can put it into practice. The exception is the sage, who takes on the challenges of a calamity the way the weak and soft takes on the tough and strong. Such a sage ruler deserves to be the leader of society and the world.

Perhaps the most important statement in this chapter is the last line, "A truthful statement sounds like its opposite," because it provides the key to understanding Laozi's favorite mode of expression, namely, the paradox.

79

和大怨，必有余怨；报怨以德，安可以为善？

是以圣人执左契，而不责于人。有德司契，无德司彻。

天道无亲，常与善人。

和大怨	If you try to reconcile major grievances
必有餘怨	There are bound to be remnants of grievances.
報怨以德	If you repay grievance with kindness,
安可以爲善	What good could that do?
是以聖人執左契	Therefore the sage keeps the receipt
而不責於人	But does not press the debtor.
有德司契	Those who have *De* are like the creditor;
無德司徹	Those who do not have *De* are like the debt collector.
天道無親	The way of Heaven is impartial,
常與善人	But it stays consistently with good people.

COMMENTARY

The third line of the first stanza, "repay grievance with kindness," is moved here from chapter 63 because it is considered by many commentators as misplaced in the received version. The whole stanza suggests that instead of trying to make amends for existing grievances, the best policy is not to cause grievances in the first place.

In Laozi's time, a loan contract was written on a bamboo slip, which was split down the middle into two halves, the lender keeping the left half and the borrower the other half (some think it was the other way round). The part the lender kept was a receipt or IOU with which he could press for payment. According to Laozi, a creditor who has attained *De* does not forgive the debt because he is "impartial" like *Dao*, but he does not press for payment either because that is the job of a debt collector who has not attained *De*. By holding on to the receipt, he tacitly reminds the debtor to honor his promise when he is ready. That is far more effective a resolution than a simple gesture of "repaying grievance with kindness."

80

小国寡民。使有什伯之器而不用；使民重死而不远徙。虽有舟舆，无所乘之；虽有甲兵，无所陈之。使民复结绳而用之。

甘其食，美其服，安其居，乐其俗。邻国相望，鸡犬之声相闻，民至老死，不相往来。

小國寡民	Let the states be small and the population be sparse.
使有什伯之器而不用	Let them have no use for mass-scale tools and utensils;
使民重死而不遠徙	Let the common people fear death and not move far.
雖有舟輿	Although boats and carriages are available,
無所乘之	Let there be no occasion to travel in them.
雖有甲兵	Although there are armors and weapons,
無所陳之	Let there be no place to store them.
使民復結繩而用之	Let people restore the skill of knotting and put it to use.
甘其食	Let them enjoy their food,
美其服	Admire their clothing,
安其居	Feel secure in their dwelling,
樂其俗	Rejoice in their culture.
鄰國相望	Let them see each other across the borders,
雞犬之聲相聞	Hear each other's roosters and dogs,
民至老死	But, till they die in ripe old age,
不相往來	Never visit each other.

COMMENTARY ....

In this penultimate chapter Laozi paints a picture of his Daoist utopia in verse. Considering the turmoil and war, the poverty and hunger, the greed and strife that permeate the world he lived in, one can feel the deep compassion and yearning that come through his poetic lines. His is a dream for peace and simplicity, a land where *Dao* prevails and people all live in harmony and content.

"Mass-scale utensils and tools" such as huge cauldrons, big boats, and carriages, already existed in Laozi's time. But he hoped small communities in his dreamland would have no use for such things. He wished the people there would take life and death seriously and not waste their energy traveling. At the same time he wanted people to unlearn all the knowledge that had clogged their minds and just be happy with the primitive technology of knotting to keep tally of simple items before writing was invented.

81

信言不美，美言不信。善者不辩，辩者不善。知者不博，博者不知。圣人不积，既以为人己愈有，既以与人己愈多。天之道，利而不害；圣人之道，为而不争。

信言不美	Truthful words are not beautiful;
美言不信	Beautiful words are not truthful.
善者不辩	One who is good is not eloquent;
辩者不善	One who is eloquent is up to no good.
知者不博	One who knows is not erudite;
博者不知	One who is erudite does not know.
聖人不積	The sage does not hoard.
既以爲人己愈有	The more he serves the more he has;
既以與人己愈多	The more he gives the more he receives.
天之道	The way of Heaven
利而不害	Brings benefits and does no harm;
聖人之道	The way of the sage
爲而不爭	Only serves and never contends.

COMMENTARY

One may never know if Laozi intended this to be his final chapter. But in a "world of thought" where "a hundred schools contend," he is reminding us, before we close these pages, not to be deceived by beautiful words, glib eloquence, and scholastic erudition. He urges us to stay with the true, the good, and the wise. As in chapter 56, the character 知 (*zhī* or *zhì*) in classical Chinese can be both the verb "to know" and the adjective "wise." The latter would in time take the form of 智 (*zhì*). So the lines "One who knows is not erudite; one who is erudite does not know" may also be read as "One who is wise is not erudite; one who is erudite is not wise." Laozi's teachings are applicable to those who govern as well as those who are governed. He is not out to gain but to give, not to harm but to benefit, not to contend but to serve.

Appendix

Chinese Glossary Index
(The numbers indicate the chapters in which the term occurs.)

道 *Dao* (The Way)

1, 4, 8, 9, 14, 15, 16, 18, 21, 23, 24, 25, 30, 31, 32, 34, 35, 37, 38, 40, 41, 42, 46, 47, 48,
51, 53, 55, 59, 60, 62, 65, 73, 77, 79, 81

德 *De* (Attainment/Virtue)

10, 21, 23, 28, 38, 39 (得), 41, 49, 51, 54, 55, 56 (得), 59, 60, 65, 68, 79

一 (One)

10, 11, 14, 22, 39, 42

母 (Mother)

1, 20, 25, 52, 59

无为 *Wuwei* (Non-doing)

2, 3, 10, 29, 37, 38, 43, 48, 57, 63, 64

柔弱 The Soft and the Weak

3, 10, 36, 40, 43, 52, 55, 76, 78

不争 Non-Contention

8, 22, 66, 68, 73, 81

圣人 The Sage

2, 3, 5, 7, 12, 22, 26, 27, 28, 29, 47, 49, 51, 58, 60, 63, 64, 66, 70, 71, 72, 73, 77, 78, 79, 81

Books Consulted

Primary Texts in Chinese:

陈鼓应. 老子注释及评介. 修订增补本. 北京: 中华书局, 2009年.
(Chen, Guying. *Laozi: Texts, Notes, and Comments.* Rev. ed. Beijing: Zhonghua
  Shuju, 2009.)

任继愈. 老子绎读. 北京: 北京图书馆出版社, 2006年.
(Ren, Jiyu. *Laozi, an Interpretive Reading.* Beijing: Beijing Library Press,
  2006.)

王卡点校. 老子道德经河上公章句. 北京: 中华书局, 1993年.
(Wang, Ka, ed. *Laozi's Dao De Jing with He Shang Gong's Line-by-Line
  Commentaries.* Beijing: Zhonghua Shuju, 1993.)

English Translations:

Ames, Roger T., and David L. Hall. *Dao De Jing: "Making This Life
  Significant": A Philosophical Translation.* New York: Ballantine Books,
  2003.

Chan, Wing-tsi. *The Way of Lao Tzu (Tao-te ching).* New York: Bobbs-Merrill
  Company, 1963.

Chen, Ellen M. *The Tao Te Ching: A New Translation with Commentary.* New
  York: Paragon House, 1989.

Cheng, Man-jan. *Lao-Tzu: "My Words Are Easy to Understand": Lectures
  on the Tao Te Ching.* Trans. Tam C. Gibbs. Richmond, CA: North Atlantic
  Books, 1981.

de Bary, Wm. Theodore, and Irene Bloom, eds. *Sources of Chinese Tradition
  from Earliest Times to 1600.* 2nd ed. New York: Columbia University Press,
  1999.

Dyer, Wayne W. *Change Your Thoughts, Change Your Life*: *Living the Wisdom of the Tao*. Carlsbad, CA: Hay House, 2007.

Feng, Gai-fu, and Jane English. *Lao Tsu: Tao Te Ching*. New York: Vintage Books, 1972.

Henricks, Robert G. *Lao-tzu: Te-Tao Ching*: *A New Translation Based on the Recently Discovered Ma-wang-tui Texts*. New York: Ballantine Books, 1989.

Lafargue, Michael. *The Tao of the Tao Te Ching*. Albany: State University of New York Press, 1992.

Lau, D. C. *Lao Tzu: Tao Te Ching*. London: Penguin Classics, 1963.

Le Guin, Ursula K. *Lao Tzu: Tao Te Ching*: *A Book about the Way and the Power of the Way*. Boston: Shambhala, 1997.

Lin, Yutang. *The Wisdom of Laotse*. New York: Random House, 1948.

Lynn, Richard John. *The Classic of Way and Virtue: A New Translation of the Tao-te ching of Laozi as Interpreted by Wang Bi*. New York: Columbia University Press, 1999.

Red Pine. *Lao-tzu's Taoteching*. San Francisco: Mercury House, 1996.

Roberts, Moss. *Laozi: Dao De Jing: The Book of the Way*. Berkeley: University of California Press, 2001.

Ryden, Edmund. *Laozi Daodejing*. Oxford: Oxford University Press, 2008.

Star, Jonathan. *Tao Te Ching: The Definitive Edition*. New York: Jeremy P. Tarcher/Penguin, 2001.

Waley, Arthur. *The Way and Its Power: A Study of the Tao Te Ching and Its Place in Chinese Thought*. New York: Grove Press, 1958.

About the Translator

Dr. Charles Q. Wu, Professor Emeritus of Chinese and Humanities at Reed College, was born and raised in Shanghai, China. He went to college at Beijing Foreign Languages Institute (now Beijing Foreign Studies University) in 1951 and graduated as an English major in 1954. He then took three years of graduate studies under the tutelage of Professors Shui Tiantong, Wang Zuoliang, and Xu Guozhang. He joined the English faculty of his alma mater in 1957. He was for many years one of the chief editors of the nationwide *English Language Learning* magazine. From 1972 to 1977, he served on the editorial board of the *Chinese-English Dictionary* (1978). In 1980 he went to Columbia University for graduate studies in English literature and earned a PhD in 1987. His doctoral dissertation was a Daoist reading of the English romantic poet William Wordsworth.

Dr. Wu then turned his interest from English literature to Chinese culture. He taught Chinese language, literature, and civilization at Reed College from 1987 to 2002. Off campus he gave public lectures on traditional Chinese culture and led study tours from the United States to China. The year 2000 saw the completion and opening of Lan Su Yuan, a classical, Suzhou-style Chinese garden in Portland, Oregon, built jointly by Portland and its sister city Suzhou. As its cultural advisor, Dr. Wu played an instrumental role in the interpretation of its cultural meanings. His book *Listen to the Fragrance* (2006) is a full translation and detailed explication of the poetic inscriptions in that garden.

Dr. Wu's new book, *Thus Spoke Laozi*, draws its strength from his excellent bilingual skills and cross-cultural perspective. It provides a new tool for English-speaking readers interested in classical Chinese culture as well as a case study for Chinese students of English learning to introduce Chinese classics to the English-speaking world.